# Citizenship
## PASSING THE TEST

# LITERACY SKILLS

Lynne Weintraub

New Readers Press

Citizenship: Passing the Test
Literacy Skills
ISBN 978-1-56420-890-3

Copyright © 2009 New Readers Press
New Readers Press
A Publishing Division of ProLiteracy
1320 Jamesville Avenue, Syracuse, New York 13210
www.newreaderspress.com

Printed in the United States of America
9  8  7  6  5  4  3  2

All proceeds from the sale of New Readers Press materials
support literacy programs in the United States and worldwide.

**Developmental Editor:** Paula L. Schlusberg, Mesa Crest Consulting
**Creative Director:** Andrea Woodbury
**Illustration Manager:** James P. Wallace
**Production Specialist:** Maryellen Casey
**Cover Design:** Carolyn Wallace

# Contents

# 1.

A A  A A _ _ _ _

a a  a a _ _ _ _

and

America

B B _ _ _ _ _ _

b b _ _ _ _ _ _

blue

Bill of Rights

C C _ _ _ _ _ _

c c _ _ _ _ _ _

citizen

Canada

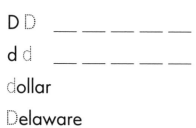

D D _ _ _ _ _ _

d d _ _ _ _ _ _

dollar

Delaware

E E _ _ _ _ _ _

e e _ _ _ _ _ _

elect

F F _ _ _ _ _ _

f f _ _ _ _ _ _

flag

February

TEACHER   For each letter: Point to, name, and have students repeat the letter and the words below the letter. Associate the letter and its sound. Reinforce this with the words pictured above, which begin with the letter. (Point out that *C* can make either of two sounds.) Have students trace and copy as indicated. Encourage students to read letters independently.

| G G _ _ _ _ _ | H H _ _ _ _ _ | I I _ _ _ _ _ |
| g g _ _ _ _ _ | h h _ _ _ _ _ | i i _ _ _ _ _ |
| government | here | is |
| George Washington | house | Indians |

| J J _ _ _ _ _ | K K _ _ _ _ _ | L L _ _ _ _ _ |
| j j _ _ _ _ _ | k k _ _ _ _ _ | l l _ _ _ _ _ |
| June | New York | law |
| July | | Lincoln |

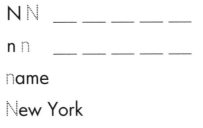

| M M _ _ _ _ _ | N N _ _ _ _ _ | O O _ _ _ _ _ |
| m m _ _ _ _ _ | n n _ _ _ _ _ | o o _ _ _ _ _ |
| meet | name | on |
| May | New York | October |

P P  _ _ _ _ _ _

p p  _ _ _ _ _ _

president

people

Q Q  _ _ _ _ _ _

q q  _ _ _ _ _ _

quarter

R R  _ _ _ _ _ _

r r  _ _ _ _ _ _

red

rights

6

S S  _ _ _ _ _ _

s s  _ _ _ _ _ _

state

September

10

T T  _ _ _ _ _ _

t t  _ _ _ _ _ _

taxes

U U  _ _ _ _ _ _

u u  _ _ _ _ _ _

United States

U.S.

V V  _ _ _ _ _ _

v v  _ _ _ _ _ _

vote

W W  _ _ _ _ _ _

w w  _ _ _ _ _ _

we

White House

**CD 1 TRACK 5  Listen. Say. Copy.**

X X  __ __ __ __ __          Y Y  __ __ __ __ __          Z Z  __ __ __ __ __

x x  __ __ __ __ __          y y  __ __ __ __ __          z z  __ __ __ __ __

tax                          day                          citizen

                             New York

**CD 1 TRACK 6  Listen. Copy.**

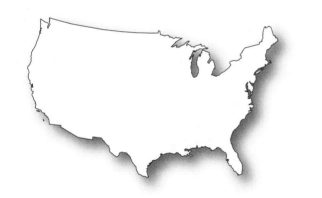

U.S.                         Washington, D.C.

__.__.                       Washington, __.__.

__.__.                       Washington, __.__.

__.__.                       Washington, __.__.

TEACHER  *Top:* Follow instructions, p. 4. *Bottom:* Point to, say, and have students repeat *U.S.* and *Washington, D.C.* Have students copy the letters on the blanks.

# 2.

| | |
|---|---|
| in | is |
| and | has |
| red | bill |
| can | flag |

TEACHER   Follow instructions for word cards in the *Teacher's Guide*, p. 45.

◎ **CD 1 TRACK 7**  Listen/Look. Listen/Say. Copy. Listen/Say.

1. **in**     i n          i n          i n

2. **is**     __ __        __ __        __ __

3. **and**    __ __ __     __ __ __     __ __ __

4. **has**    __ __ __     __ __ __     __ __ __


**Find the word.**

1. **in**     is      as      (in)      it      (in)

2. **and**    an      and     and       end     an

3. **is**     in      is      it        is      sit

4. **has**    has     hat     has       lass    ham


◎ **CD 1 TRACK 8**  Listen/Look. Listen/Say. Copy. Listen/Say.

1. **red**    __ __ __     __ __ __     __ __ __

2. **bill**   __ __ __     __ __ __     __ __ __

3. **can**    __ __ __     __ __ __     __ __ __

4. **flag**   __ __ __ __     __ __ __ __     __ __ __ __

**Find the word.**

| 1. **can** | cat | can | came | con | can |
|---|---|---|---|---|---|
| 2. **red** | red | read | net | rat | red |
| 3. **bill** | ball | bell | bill | bit | bill |
| 4. **flag** | flat | flame | flag | lag | flag |

 **CD 1 TRACK 9  Listen.**

**A a**   **E e**   **I i**

 **CD 1 TRACK 10  Listen. Write *a* or *i*.**

1. _a_nd     3. ___dams     5. ___ndian

2. ___n     4. ___s

 **CD 1 TRACK 11  Listen. Write *a*, *e*, or *i*.**

1. h___s     3. b___ll     5. fl___g

2. r___d     4. c___n

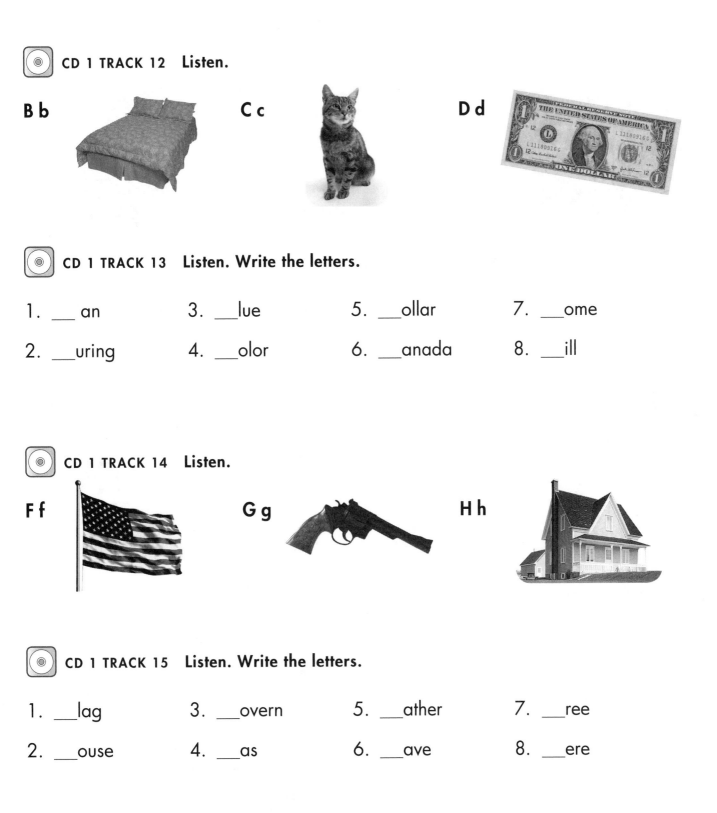

◎ **CD 1 TRACK 12**  **Listen.**

**B b**　　　　　　　　　**C c**　　　　　　　　**D d**

◎ **CD 1 TRACK 13**  **Listen. Write the letters.**

1. ___ an　　　3. ___lue　　　5. ___ollar　　　7. ___ome

2. ___uring　　4. ___olor　　　6. ___anada　　　8. ___ill

◎ **CD 1 TRACK 14**  **Listen.**

**F f**　　　　　　　　　**G g**　　　　　　　　**H h**

◎ **CD 1 TRACK 15**  **Listen. Write the letters.**

1. ___lag　　　3. ___overn　　　5. ___ather　　　7. ___ree

2. ___ouse　　4. ___as　　　　6. ___ave　　　　8. ___ere

TEACHER　Follow instructions, p. 10, center & bottom. *Words for exercises:*
*Top:* 1. can  2. during  3. blue  4. color  5. dollar  6. Canada  7. come  8. bill.
*Bottom:* 1. flag  2. house 3. govern  4. has  5. father  6. have  7. free  8. here.

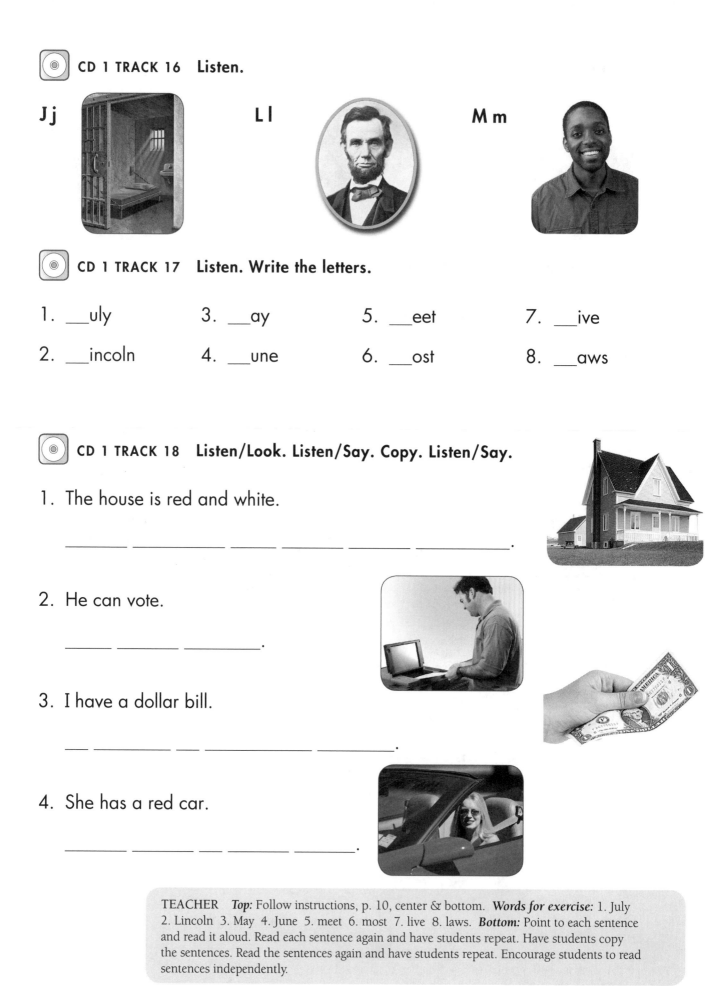

CD 1 TRACK 16  **Listen.**

J j          L l          M m

CD 1 TRACK 17  **Listen. Write the letters.**

1. __uly          3. __ay          5. __eet          7. __ive

2. __incoln       4. __une         6. __ost          8. __aws

CD 1 TRACK 18  **Listen/Look. Listen/Say. Copy. Listen/Say.**

1. The house is red and white.

   _____ _____ ___ _____ _____ _____.

2. He can vote.

   _____ _____ _____.

3. I have a dollar bill.

   __ _____ __ _____ _____.

4. She has a red car.

   _____ ____ __ _____ _____.

TEACHER   *Top:* Follow instructions, p. 10, center & bottom. ***Words for exercise:*** 1. July
2. Lincoln 3. May 4. June 5. meet 6. most 7. live 8. laws. ***Bottom:*** Point to each sentence
and read it aloud. Read each sentence again and have students repeat. Have students copy
the sentences. Read the sentences again and have students repeat. Encourage students to read
sentences independently.

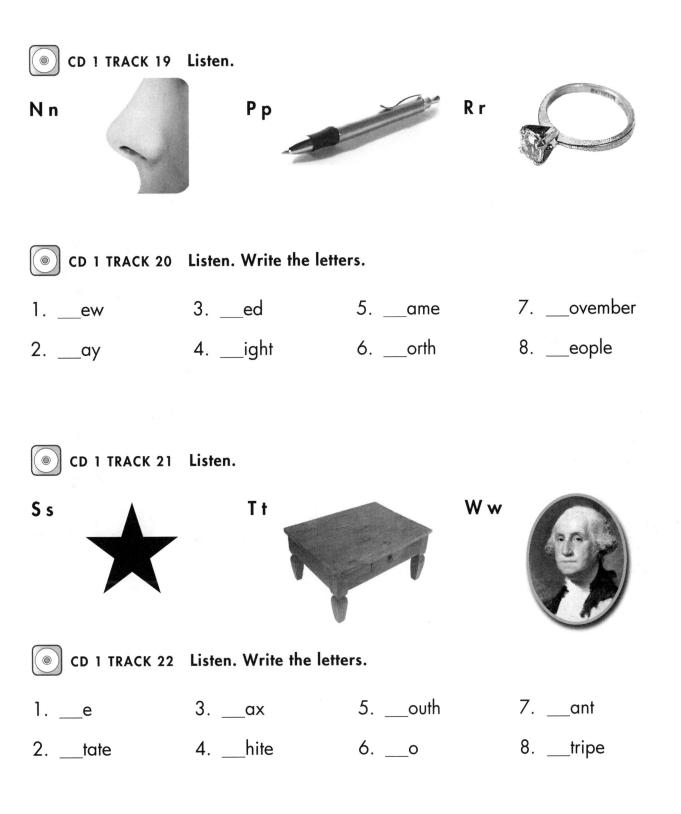

CD 1 TRACK 19 **Listen.**

**N n**  **P p**  **R r**

CD 1 TRACK 20 **Listen. Write the letters.**

1. __ew
2. __ay
3. __ed
4. __ight
5. __ame
6. __orth
7. __ovember
8. __eople

CD 1 TRACK 21 **Listen.**

**S s**  **T t**  **W w**

CD 1 TRACK 22 **Listen. Write the letters.**

1. __e
2. __tate
3. __ax
4. __hite
5. __outh
6. __o
7. __ant
8. __tripe

TEACHER   Follow instructions, p. 10, center & bottom. *Words for exercises: Top:* 1. new
2. pay  3. red  4. right  5. name  6. north  7. November  8. people. *Bottom:* 1. we  2. state
3. tax  4. white  5. south  6. to  7. want  8. stripe.

1. _____ 2. _____ 3. _____ 4. _____

💿 **CD 1 TRACK 24** **Listen/Look. Listen/Say. Copy. Listen/Say.**

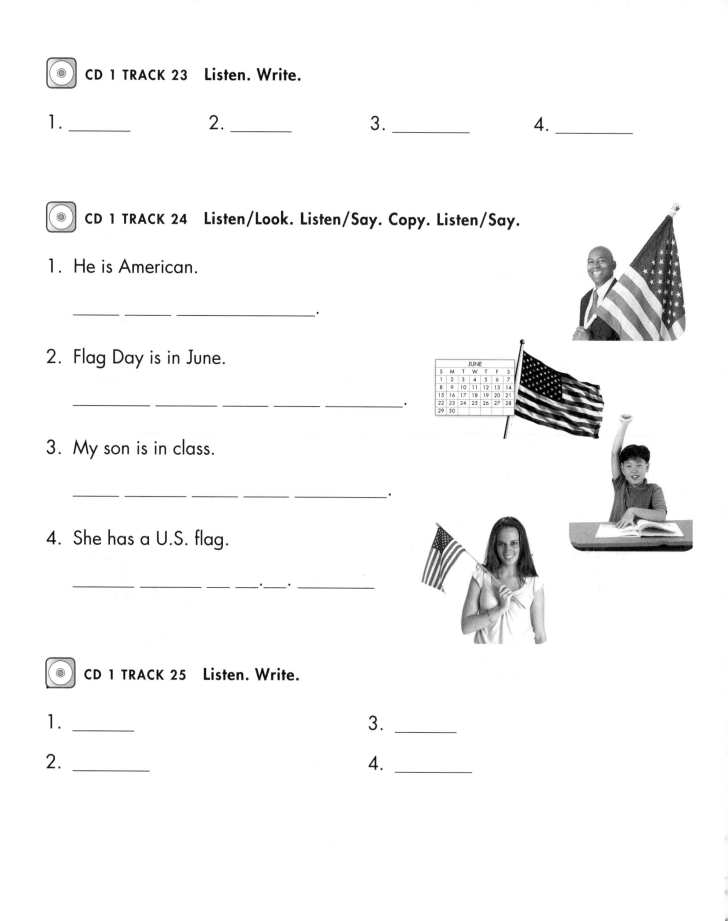

1. He is American.

   _____ _____ _____.

2. Flag Day is in June.

   _____ _____ _____ _____ _____.

3. My son is in class.

   _____ _____ _____ _____ _____.

4. She has a U.S. flag.

   _____ _____ ___ __.__. _____

💿 **CD 1 TRACK 25** **Listen. Write.**

1. _____   3. _____

2. _____   4. _____

TEACHER   *Top: Spelling quiz:* Read these words (several times, slowly) as students write them: 1. in 2. is 3. and 4. has. **Center:** Follow instructions, p. 12, bottom. ***Bottom:** Spelling quiz:* Read these words (several times, slowly) as students write them: 1. can 2. red 3. bill 4. flag.

**CD 1 TRACK 26  Listen. Write the words.**

1. The house is red _____ white.

2. He _____ vote.

3. I have a dollar _____.

4. She _____ a _____ car.

5. He _____ American.

6. _____ Day is _____ June.

7. My son is _____ class.

8. She _____ a __.___. flag.

TEACHER  *Dictation:* Read the sentences (several times, slowly) as students write the missing words on the lines: 1. The house is red and white.  2. He can vote.  3. I have a dollar bill.  4. She has a red car.  5. He is American.  6. Flag Day is in June.  7. My son is in class.  8. She has a U.S. flag.

# 3.

state

make

here

white

stripe

vote

June

TEACHER   Follow instructions for word cards in the *Teacher's Guide*, p. 45.

**16**   Section 3

1. **state** \_\_ \_\_ \_\_ \_\_ \_\_    \_\_ \_\_ \_\_ \_\_ \_\_    \_\_ \_\_ \_\_ \_\_ \_\_

2. **make** \_\_ \_\_ \_\_ \_\_    \_\_ \_\_ \_\_ \_\_    \_\_ \_\_ \_\_ \_\_

3. **here** \_\_ \_\_ \_\_ \_\_    \_\_ \_\_ \_\_ \_\_    \_\_ \_\_ \_\_ \_\_

4. **name** \_\_ \_\_ \_\_ \_\_    \_\_ \_\_ \_\_ \_\_    \_\_ \_\_ \_\_ \_\_

**Find the word.**

| | | | | | |
|---|---|---|---|---|---|
| 1. **state** | stay | state | say | state | slate |
| 2. **name** | name | nape | none | mane | name |
| 3. **make** | made | make | mad | make | maze |
| 4. **here** | hare | here | here | her | neat |

1. **white** \_\_ \_\_ \_\_ \_\_ \_\_    \_\_ \_\_ \_\_ \_\_ \_\_    \_\_ \_\_ \_\_ \_\_ \_\_

2. **stripe** \_\_ \_\_ \_\_ \_\_ \_\_ \_\_    \_\_ \_\_ \_\_ \_\_ \_\_ \_\_    \_\_ \_\_ \_\_ \_\_ \_\_ \_\_

3. **vote** \_\_ \_\_ \_\_ \_\_    \_\_ \_\_ \_\_ \_\_    \_\_ \_\_ \_\_ \_\_

4. **June** \_\_ \_\_ \_\_ \_\_    \_\_ \_\_ \_\_ \_\_    \_\_ \_\_ \_\_ \_\_

TEACHER   Follow instructions, p. 9, top & center.

# Find the word.

1. **white**     when     while     white     wine     white

2. **stripe**     strip     stripe     sting     stripe     spite

3. **vote**     veal     vase     vote     vote     wrote

4. **June**     June     July     June     Jan     Jen

## Circle: <u>stripes</u>

## Circle: <u>white</u>

TEACHER   *Top:* Follow instructions, p. 9, center. **Bottom:** In each *Circle* exercise, read the underlined word and have students circle the corresponding picture. The first one is done as a model for students.

◉ CD 1 TRACK 29   Listen.

**a**te                          **a**ke                          **e**re

◉ CD 1 TRACK 30   Listen. Write the letters.

1. st__t__                2. h__r__                3. m__k__

◉ CD 1 TRACK 31   Listen/Look. Listen/Say. Copy. Listen/Say.

1. Their flag has a stripe.

   _____ _____ ___ __ _____.

2. New York is a U.S. state.

   _____ _____ ___ __ __.__. _____.

3. They make U.S. flags.

   _____ _____ __.__. _____.

◉ CD 1 TRACK 32   Listen.

**i**te                **i**pe                **o**te                **u**ne

TEACHER   *Top:* Pronounce the sound made by each set of letters. Emphasize that the *e* does not make any sound on the ends of words with these patterns. *Next:* Read the following words and have students fill in the missing letters. Refer to the spelling patterns above: 1. state  2. here  3. make. *Center:* Follow instructions, p. 12, bottom. *Bottom:* Follow instructions for top of page.

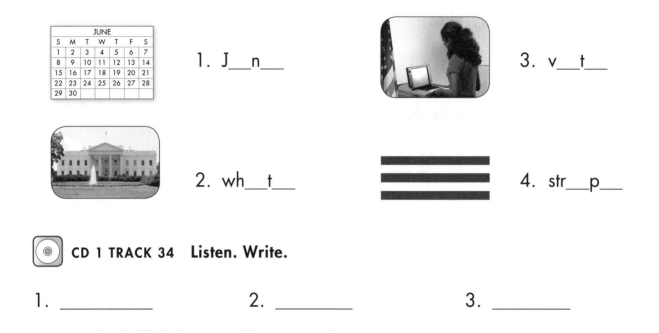

**CD 1 TRACK 33** **Listen. Write the letters.**

1. J__n__

2. wh__t__

3. v__t__

4. str__p__

**CD 1 TRACK 34** **Listen. Write.**

1. _____

2. _____

3. _____

**CD 1 TRACK 35** **Listen/Look. Listen/Say. Copy. Listen/Say.**

1. We live here.

_____ _____ _____.

2. He can vote.

_____ _____ _____.

3. Our house is white.

_____ _____ _____ _____.

4. Flag Day is in June.

_____ _____ _____ _____ _____.

1. _____             3. _____

2. _____           4. _____

🎧 CD 1 TRACK 37    **Listen. Write the words.**

1. We live _____.

2. Their _____ _____ a _____.

3. _____ Day _____ _____ _____.

4. Our house _____ _____.

5. They _____ flags.

6. New York _____ a U.S. _____.

7. He _____ _____.

TEACHER    *Top: Spelling quiz:* Read these words (several times, slowly) as students write them: 1. white   2. stripe   3. vote   4. June.   **Bottom: Dictation:** Read the sentences (several times, slowly) as students write the missing words on the lines: 1. We live here.   2. Their flag has a stripe.   3. Flag Day is in June.   4. Our house is white.   5. They make flags.   6. New York is a U.S. state.   7. He can vote.

# 4.

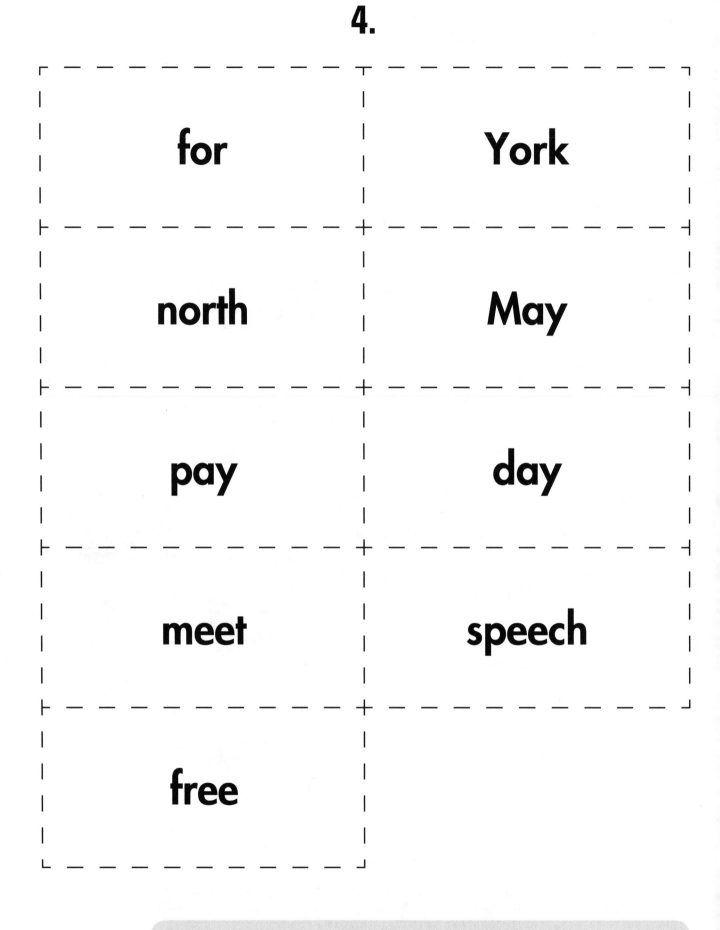

| for | York |
|-----|------|
| north | May |
| pay | day |
| meet | speech |
| free | |

TEACHER   Follow instructions for word cards in the *Teacher's Guide*, p. 45.

**CD 1 TRACK 38**   Listen/Look. Listen/Say. Copy. Listen/Say.

1. **May**     __ __ __     __ __ __     __ __ __

2. **pay**     __ __ __     __ __ __     __ __ __

3. **day**     __ __ __     __ __ __     __ __ __

**Find the word.**

| | | | | | |
|---|---|---|---|---|---|
| 1. **May** | Man | Nag | May | Many | May |
| 2. **pay** | pad | pay | bay | pay | dye |
| 3. **day** | day | date | ray | dad | day |

**CD 1 TRACK 39**   Listen/Look. Listen/Say. Copy. Listen/Say.

1. **meet**     __ __ __ __     __ __ __ __     __ __ __ __

2. **free**     __ __ __ __     __ __ __ __     __ __ __ __

3. **speech**     __ __ __ __ __ __     __ __ __ __ __ __     __ __ __ __ __ __

Follow instructions, p. 9, top & center.

**Find the word.**

1. **meet**    mean    meet    met    team    meet

2. **free**    fee    fret    free    free    tree

3. **speech**    speech    spend    spree    speech    spear

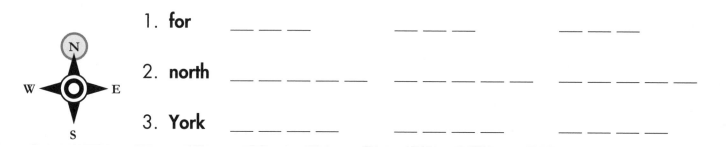

CD 1 TRACK 40    Listen/Look. Listen/Say. Copy. Listen/Say.

1. **for**    _ _ _        _ _ _        _ _ _

2. **north**    _ _ _ _ _        _ _ _ _ _        _ _ _ _ _

3. **York**    _ _ _ _        _ _ _ _        _ _ _ _

**Find the word.**

1. **for**    for    foot    for    from    nor

2. **north**    forth    north    norm    north    nor

3. **York**    York    Yoke    Your    Yolk    York

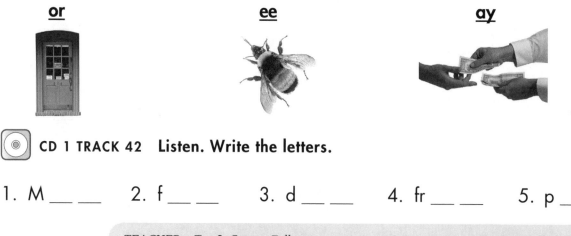

CD 1 TRACK 41    Listen.

<u>or</u>            <u>ee</u>            <u>ay</u>

CD 1 TRACK 42    Listen. Write the letters.

1. M _ _        2. f _ _        3. d _ _        4. fr _ _        5. p _ _

TEACHER    *Top & Center:* Follow instructions, p. 9, top & center. ***Bottom:*** Follow instructions, p. 19, next. Associate the letters and sounds with the pictured words. *Words for exercise:* 1. May 2. for  3. day  4. free  5. pay.

**CD 1 TRACK 43**   Listen/Look. Listen/Say. Copy. Listen/Say.

1. They came in May.

   _____ _____ _____ _____.

2. We can meet here.

   _____ _____ _____ _____.

3. New York is a state.

   _____ _____ _____ ___ _____.

4. We pay taxes.

   _____ _____ _____.

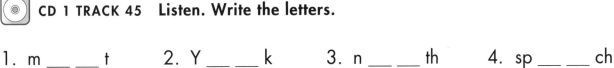

**CD 1 TRACK 44**   Listen.

<u>or</u>

<u>ee</u>

**CD 1 TRACK 45**   Listen. Write the letters.

1. m __ __ t      2. Y __ __ k      3. n __ __ th      4. sp __ __ ch

**CD 1 TRACK 46   Listen. Write.**

1. _____     2. _____     3. _____     4. _____

**CD 1 TRACK 47   Listen/Look. Listen/Say. Copy. Listen/Say.**

1. He lives in the north.

   _____ _____ ____ _____ _____.

2. They are free for a day.

   _____ _____ __ _____ __ _____.

3. She is making a speech.

   _____ ____ _____ __ _____.

**CD 1 TRACK 48   Listen. Write.**

1. _____          4. _____

2. _____      5. _____

3. _____

**CD 1 TRACK 49  Listen. Write the words.**

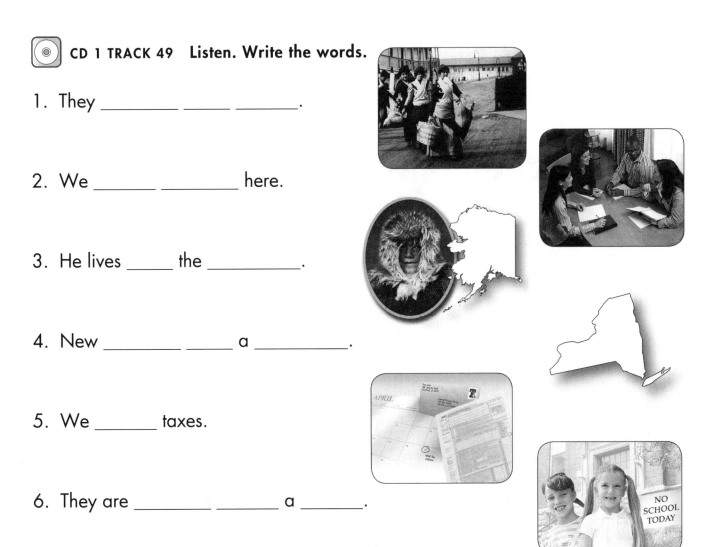

1. They _____ _____ _____.

2. We _____ _____ here.

3. He lives _____ the _____.

4. New _____ _____ a _____.

5. We _____ taxes.

6. They are _____ _____ a _____.

TEACHER  *Dictation:* 1. They came in May.  2. We can meet here.  3. He lives in the north.
4. New York is a state.  5. We pay taxes.  6. They are free for a day.

# 5.

| | |
|---|---|
| father | thank |
| first | the |
| they | most |
| one | house |
| south | war |

TEACHER   Follow instructions for word cards in the *Teacher's Guide*, p. 45.

**28**   Section 5

**CD 1 TRACK 50**  Listen/Look. Listen/Say. Copy. Listen/Say.

1. **the**  ___ ___ ___   ___ ___ ___   ___ ___ ___

2. **they**  ___ ___ ___ ___   ___ ___ ___ ___   ___ ___ ___ ___

3. **thanks**  ___ ___ ___ ___ ___ ___   ___ ___ ___ ___ ___ ___   ___ ___ ___ ___ ___ ___

4. **father**  ___ ___ ___ ___ ___ ___   ___ ___ ___ ___ ___ ___   ___ ___ ___ ___ ___ ___

**CD 1 TRACK 51**  Look. Listen. Copy.

1. house

___ ___ ___ ___ ___

___ ___ ___ ___ ___

___ ___ ___ ___ ___

2. pay

___ ___ ___

___ ___ ___

___ ___ ___

3. meet

___ ___ ___ ___

___ ___ ___ ___

___ ___ ___ ___

4. flag

___ ___ ___ ___

___ ___ ___ ___

___ ___ ___ ___

5. south

___ ___ ___ ___ ___

___ ___ ___ ___ ___

___ ___ ___ ___ ___

6. north

___ ___ ___ ___ ___

___ ___ ___ ___ ___

___ ___ ___ ___ ___

7. war

___ ___ ___

___ ___ ___

___ ___ ___

8. one

___ ___ ___

___ ___ ___

___ ___ ___

TEACHER  *Top:* Follow instructions, p. 9, top. *Bottom:* Have students look at the picture and listen as you read each word. Then have students copy the words.

**Find the word.**

1. **the**      this     the     three     them     the

2. **thanks**    thinks    thanks    than    thanks    thin

3. **father**    favor    tether    father    feather    father

4. **they**     the    them    they    they    hey

5. **one**      on    one    one    none    noon

**CD 1 TRACK 52**   **Listen/Look. Listen/Say. Copy. Listen/Say.**

1. **our**   ___ ___ ___      ___ ___ ___      ___ ___ ___

2. **house**   ___ ___ ___ ___     ___ ___ ___ ___     ___ ___ ___ ___

3. **south**   ___ ___ ___ ___     ___ ___ ___ ___     ___ ___ ___ ___

4. **most**   ___ ___ ___     ___ ___ ___     ___ ___ ___

5. **first**   ___ ___ ___ ___     ___ ___ ___ ___     ___ ___ ___ ___

TEACHER   *Top:* Follow instructions, p. 9, center.  *Bottom:* Follow instructions, p. 9, top.

**Match.**

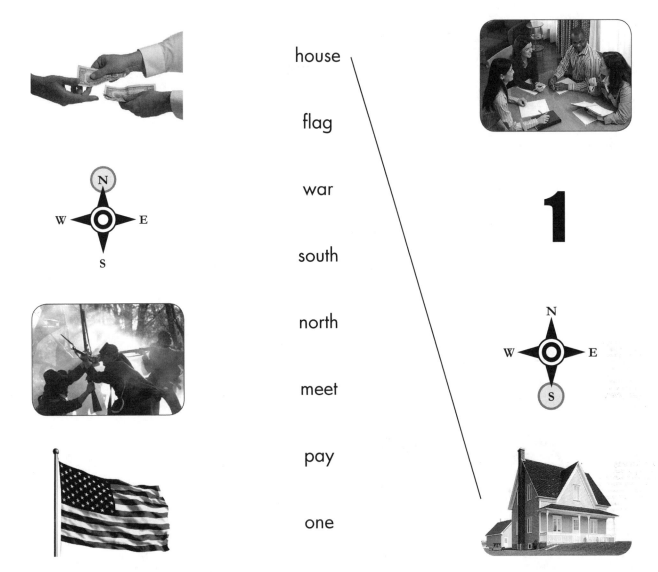

house

flag

war

south

north

meet

pay

one

1

**Circle: Who is first?**

TEACHER   *Top:* Read (or have students read) each word on the list. Help students match each word (draw a line) to the corresponding picture. The first one is done as a model for students.
*Bottom:* Read the question and have students circle the first person in the line.

**Find the word.**

| | | | | | |
|---|---|---|---|---|---|
| 1. **our** | our | out | ouch | our | sour |
| 2. **south** | sound | south | south | spout | mouth |
| 3. **house** | hound | house | hour | house | hose |
| 4. **first** | first | fist | first | firm | fast |
| 5. **most** | mist | most | must | most | moss |
| 6. **war** | warn | war | were | war | wear |
| 7. **one** | on | one | only | one | won |

**Circle: Who has the <u>most</u>?**

TEACHER  *Top:* Follow instructions, p. 9, center. *Bottom:* Read the question and have students circle the person holding the most books.

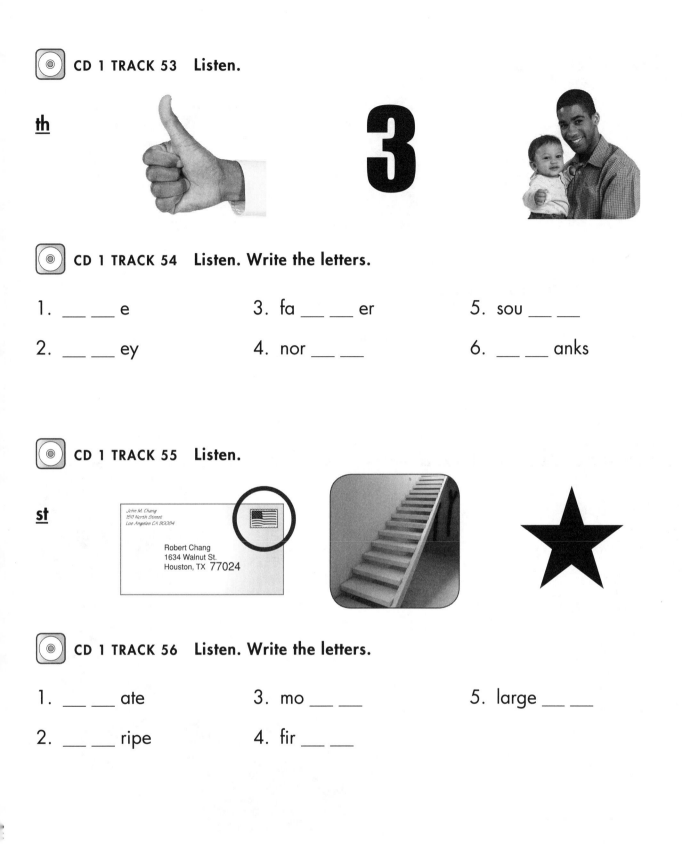

**CD 1 TRACK 53**  **Listen.**

<u>th</u>

**CD 1 TRACK 54**  **Listen. Write the letters.**

1. __ __ e

2. __ __ ey

3. fa __ __ er

4. nor __ __

5. sou __ __

6. __ __ anks

**CD 1 TRACK 55**  **Listen.**

<u>st</u>

**CD 1 TRACK 56**  **Listen. Write the letters.**

1. __ __ ate

2. __ __ ripe

3. mo __ __

4. fir __ __

5. large __ __

TEACHER  *Top:* Point to the letters *th* and pronounce the two sounds of *th.* Say each pictured word: *thumb, three, father.* Read the following words and have students fill in the missing letters: 1. the 2. they 3. father 4. north 5. south 6. thanks. *Bottom:* Follow instructions for top of page. Say: *stamp, stairs, star.* Words for exercise: 1. state 2. stripe 3. month 4. first 5. largest.

◎ **CD 1 TRACK 57   Listen.**

**<u>ou</u>**

◎ **CD 1 TRACK 58   Listen. Write the letters.**

1. __ __ r          2. h __ __ se          3. s __ __ th

◎ **CD 1 TRACK 59   Listen/Look. Listen/Say. Copy. Listen/Say.**

1. My father is in New York.

_____ _____ _____ _____ _____ _____.

2. Indians lived here first.

_____ _____ _____ _____.

3. Her house is red.

_____ _____ _____ _____.

**TEACHER**   *Top:* Point to the letters *ou* and pronounce the "ou" sound as in *house.* Say each pictured word: *south, house, cloud.* Read the following words and have students fill in the missing letters: 1. our  2. house  3. south. ***Bottom:*** Follow instructions, p. 12, bottom.

CD 1 TRACK 60 **Listen. Write.**

1. _____   3. _____   5. _____

2. _____   4. _____

**Write the word.**

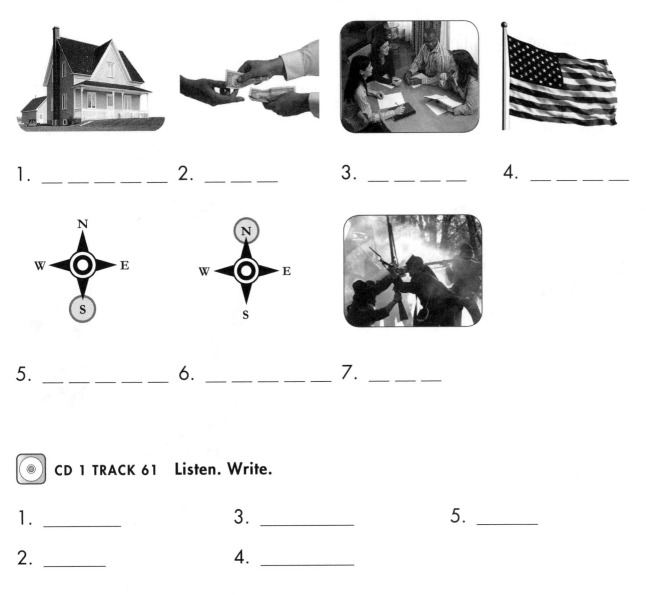

1. __ __ __ __   2. __ __ __   3. __ __ __ __   4. __ __ __ __

5. __ __ __ __ __   6. __ __ __ __ __ __   7. __ __ __

CD 1 TRACK 61 **Listen. Write.**

1. _____   3. _____   5. _____

2. _____   4. _____

*Top:* *Spelling quiz:* 1. father  2. thank  3. first  4. the  5. they. *Center:* Help students identify each picture and write the word. *Bottom:* Spelling quiz: 1. most  2. our  3. house  4. south  5. war.

**CD 1 TRACK 62** **Listen/Look. Listen/Say. Copy. Listen/Say.**

1. Most people pay taxes.

   _____ _____ _____ _____.

2. They live in the south.

   _____ _____ ____ _____ _____.

3. Thanks for the flag.

   _____ _____ ____ _____.

4. He was in the war.

   _____ _____ ____ _____ _____.

**CD 1 TRACK 63** **Listen. Write the words.**

1. My _____ is in New _____.

2. Indians lived _____ _____.

3. Her _____ is _____.

4. _____ people _____ taxes.

5. _____ live in _____ _____.

6. _____ _____ the _____.

7. He was in _____ _____.

TEACHER  *Top:* Follow instructions, p. 12, bottom. ***Bottom:*** *Dictation:* 1. My father is in New York.  2. Indians lived here first.  3. Her house is red.  4. Most people pay taxes.  5. They live in the south.  6. Thanks for the flag.  7. He was in the war.

**CD 1 TRACK 64** **Listen/Say.**

### Read-alouds

1.  Name one war.

2.  Name one state.

3.  Name a state in the South.

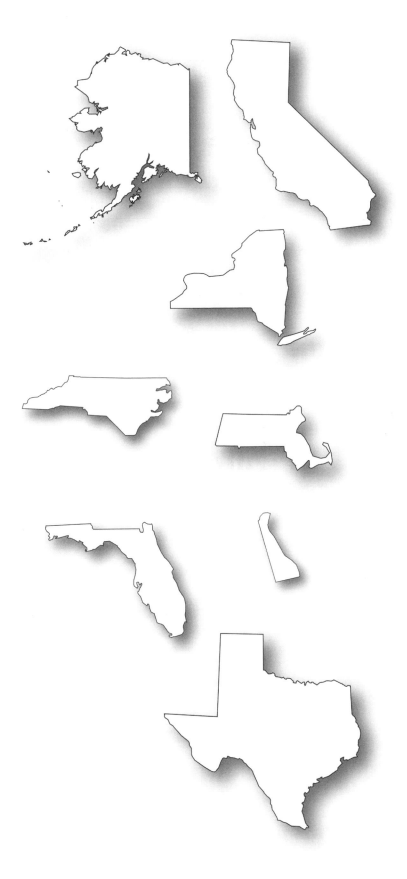

TEACHER   Point to each sentence and model reading it for students. Have students try to read each sentence aloud.

Section 5   **37**

# 6.

be

we

to

New

blue

TEACHER   Follow instructions for word cards in the *Teacher's Guide,* p. 45.

1. **to** ___ ___          ___ ___          ___ ___

2. **do** ___ ___          ___ ___          ___ ___

3. **New** ___ ___ ___      ___ ___ ___      ___ ___ ___

4. **blue** ___ ___ ___ ___   ___ ___ ___ ___   ___ ___ ___ ___

◉ **CD 1 TRACK 66** **Sound-alikes**

| to | Who | New |  |
|----|-----|-----|---|
| do | blue | | |

**Copy on the lines.**

red, white, and blue

_____, white, _____ blue

red, _____, and _____

_____, white, _____ _____

_____, _____, _____ _____

TEACHER   *Top:* Follow instructions, p. 9, top.   *Center:* Point to each word/picture in the first row. Say: *to, Who, New, shoe.* Ask students, *"What sound do you hear in each of these words?"* Point to each word/picture in the second row. Say: *do, blue, screw, two.* Ask the same question. Explain that there are many ways to spell the "oo" sound in English. Help students identify which letters make the "oo" sound in each word.   *Bottom:* Help students read the phrase *red, white, and blue* aloud, then copy the words onto the blanks.

**Circle: <u>new</u>**

**Circle: <u>New York</u>**

**Find the word.**

| 1. **do** | do | dot | dog | do | does |
| 2. **to** | toy | top | toe | to | to |
| 3. **who** | who | whom | woe | who | what |
| 4. **blue** | blow | blue | blue | due | blue |
| 5. **New** | New | Newt | Net | Now | New |

◉ **CD 1 TRACK 67   Listen/Look. Listen/Say. Copy. Listen/Say.**

1. **be**   __ __      __ __      __ __

2. **we**   __ __      __ __      __ __

TEACHER   *Top:* Follow instructions, p. 18, bottom.  *Center:* Follow instructions, p. 9, center.
*Bottom:* Follow instructions, p. 9, top.

**CD 1 TRACK 68   Sound-alikes.**

be

we

**3**

## Find the word.

1. **be**       be       bet       be       beg       be

2. **we**       went       we       wet       we       web

## Circle: Who is <u>on</u> the house?

## Circle: Who has a <u>flag</u>?

TEACHER   *Top:* Follow instructions, p. 39, center. First row, say: *be, bee, tea, three.* Second row, say: *we, key, tree.* Help students identify which letters make the "ee" sound in each word. *Center:* Follow instructions, p. 9, center. *Bottom:* Read each question. Help students find and circle the corresponding picture.

**Find sound-alikes.**

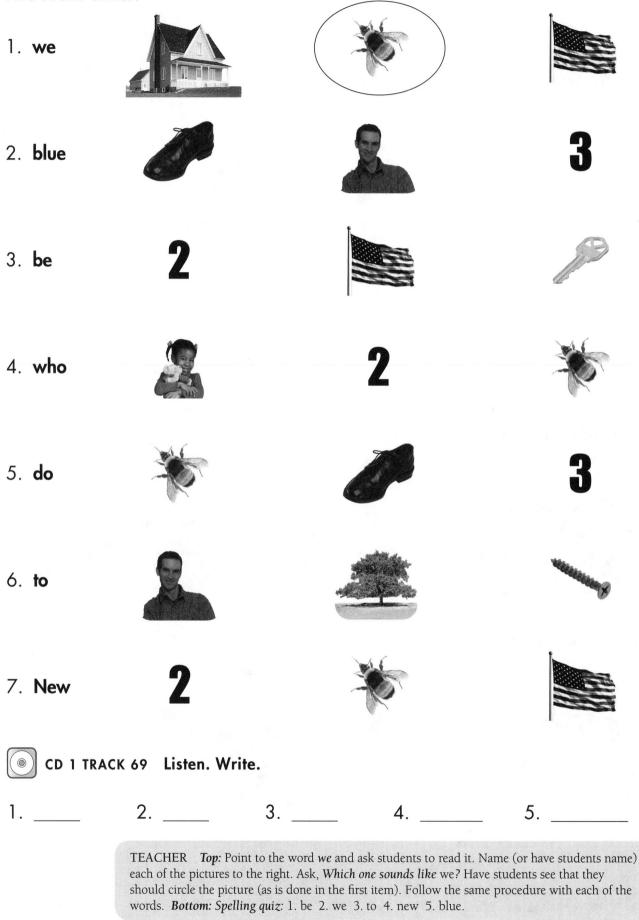

1. we

2. blue

3. be

4. who

5. do

6. to

7. New

CD 1 TRACK 69   Listen. Write.

1. _____   2. _____   3. _____   4. _____   5. _____

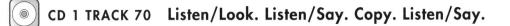

**⊚ CD 1 TRACK 70**   Listen/Look. Listen/Say. Copy. Listen/Say.

1. The flag is red, white, and blue.

   _____ _____ _____ _____, _____, _____ _____.

2. We live in New York.

   _____ _____ _____ _____ _____.

3. They want to be free.

   _____ _____ _____ _____ _____.

**⊚ CD 1 TRACK 71**   Listen. Write the words.

1. The _____ is _____ , white, and _____.

2. _____ live in _____ York.

3. They want _____ _____ _____.

**⊚ CD 1 TRACK 72**   Read-alouds.

1. Who can vote?

2. Who can make a flag?

3. Who can be free?

4. Who has free speech?

5. Who is in the White House?

TEACHER   *Top:* Follow instructions, p. 12, bottom.   *Center: Dictation:* 1. The flag is red, white, and blue.   2. We live in New York.   3. They want to be free.   *Bottom:* Point to each question and model reading it for students. Have students try to read each question aloud.

# 7.

of

on

was

live

TEACHER   Follow instructions for word cards in the *Teacher's Guide*, p. 45.

**44**   Section 7

Listen/Look. Listen/Say. Copy. Listen/Say.

1. **of** ___ ___          ___ ___          ___ ___

2. **on** ___ ___          ___ ___          ___ ___

3. **was** ___ ___ ___     ___ ___ ___     ___ ___ ___

4. **live** ___ ___ ___ ___   ___ ___ ___ ___   ___ ___ ___ ___

Listen. Look. Say.

1. Who     2. What     3. does     4. name     5. one

Sound-alikes.

1. **of**

2. **on**

3. **What**

4. **one**

5. **was**     **does**

Circle: What is <u>on</u> the U.S. flag?

TEACHER    *Top:* Follow instructions, p. 9, top. *Next:* Point to and read each word while students listen. Read again and have students repeat. Then have students read each word aloud. *Center:* Point to the word *of.* Say, *"Here is a word that sound like* of—glove." Ask, *"What sound do you hear in both words?"* Follow this procedure with each word. *Bottom:* Follow instructions, p. 41, bottom.

**Find the word.**

1. **of**      off      of      on      out      of

2. **on**      on      one      on      only      odd

3. **was**      wash      wand      was      was      wash

4. **live**      life      alive      live      lit      live

5. **does**      do      dose      does      does      doles

6. **What**      What      Why      What      Want      Wait

**Find sound-alikes.**

1. **of**

2. **on**

3. **What**

4. **one**

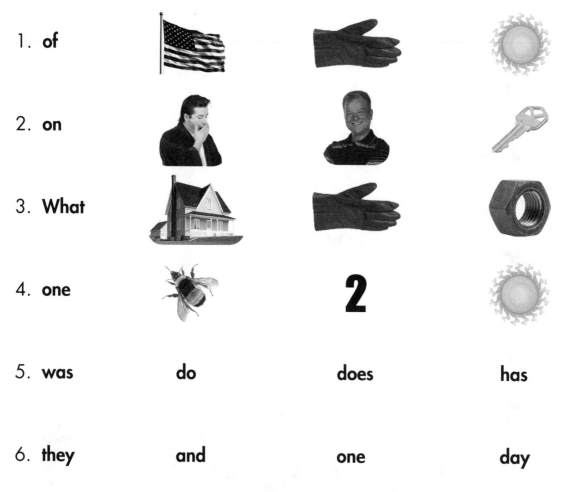

5. **was**      do      does      has

6. **they**      and      one      day

TEACHER   *Top:* Follow instructions, p. 9, center.  *Bottom:* Follow instructions, p. 42, top.

**CD 1 TRACK 76**  **Listen. Write.**

1. _____          2. _____          3. _____          4. _____

**CD 1 TRACK 77**  **Listen/Look. Listen/Say. Copy. Listen/Say.**

1. We live in the United States of America.

_____ _____ _____ _____ _____

_____ _____ _____.

2. We have freedom of speech.

_____ _____ _____ _____ _____.

3. Delaware was the first state.

_____ _____ _____ _____ _____.

4. The stripes on the flag are red and white.

_____ _____ _____ _____ _____

_____ _____ _____ _____.

TEACHER  *Top:* Spelling quiz: 1. of  2. on  3. was  4. live.  ***Bottom:*** Follow instructions, p. 12, bottom.

**CD 1 TRACK 78  Listen. Write.**

1. _____ _____ ____ _____ United States

   _____ America.

2. _____ have freedom _____ _____.

3. _____ _____ ____ _____

   _____ are _____ _____ _____.

4. Delaware _____ _____ _____ _____.

**CD 1 TRACK 79  Read-alouds**

1. What does a father do?

2. What is in the White House?

3. What do they make here?

4. What has red and white stripes?

5. What was the first state?

TEACHER   *Top: Dictation:* 1. We live in the United States of America.  2. We have freedom of speech.  3. The stripes on the flag are red and white.  4. Delaware was the first state.
*Bottom:* Follow instructions, p. 43, bottom.

# 8.

| have | are |
|------|-----|
| come | want |
| right | laws |

TEACHER   Follow instructions for word cards in the *Teacher's Guide,* p. 45.

Section 8   **49**

**CD 2 TRACK 1**   Listen/Look. Listen/Say. Copy. Listen/Say.

1. **are**    __ __ __          __ __ __          __ __ __

2. **law**    __ __ __          __ __ __          __ __ __

3. **come**   __ __ __ __       __ __ __ __       __ __ __ __

4. **want**   __ __ __ __       __ __ __ __       __ __ __ __

5. **have**   __ __ __ __       __ __ __ __       __ __ __ __

6. **right**  __ __ __ __ __    __ __ __ __ __    __ __ __ __ __

**CD 2 TRACK 2**   Sound-alikes

1. **are**

2. **laws**

3. **come**

4. **want**

5. **right**

TEACHER   *Top:* Follow instructions, p. 9, top.  ***Bottom:*** Follow instructions, p. 42, top.

**Find the word.**

1. **are**      art      arm      are      at      are
2. **laws**     laws     lawns    land     laps    laws
3. **come**     comb     cone     come     come    cob
4. **want**     want     wane     wand     want    war
5. **have**     hay      hand     have     had     have
6. **right**    ripe     right    rice     right   sight

CD 2 TRACK 3   **Listen. Look. Say.**

1. Why          3. Where          5. George
2. When         4. How

CD 2 TRACK 4   **Sound-alikes**

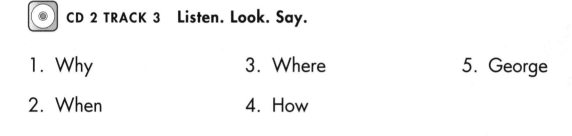
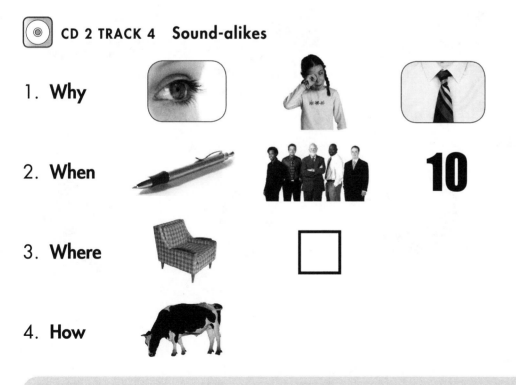

1. **Why**

2. **When**

3. **Where**

4. **How**

TEACHER   *Top:* Follow instructions, p. 9, center. *Center:* Point to and read each word while students listen. Read again and have students repeat. Then have students read each word aloud. *Bottom:* Follow instructions, p. 45, center.

**Find the word.**

1. **Why**     Way     Why     Why     White     Wash

2. **When**     Went     When     What     When     West

3. **Where**     Where     White     When     Where     Were

4. **How**     Hot     How     Home     How     Hop

5. **George**     Good     George     Group     George     Green

**Circle: When do we <u>vote</u>?**

**Circle: What flag is <u>right</u>?**

**Circle: Where is <u>George</u>?**

TEACHER   *Top:* Follow instructions, p. 9, center.   ***Bottom:*** Follow instructions, p. 41, bottom.

**52**   Section 8

# Find sound-alikes.

1. **are**

2. **come**

3. **want**

4. **right**

 **CD 2 TRACK 5   Listen. Say. Copy.**

*Bill of Rights*

Bill of Rights

_____ of Rights

Bill _____ Rights

_____ of _____

_____ _____ _____

◎ **CD 2 TRACK 6  Listen. Write.**

1. _____        3. _____        5. _____

2. _____        4. _____        6. _____


◎ **CD 2 TRACK 7  Listen/Look. Listen/Say. Copy. Listen/Say.**

1. live        lives        4. meet        meets
   live        live s              meet        meet__

   l i v e    l i v e s    _ _ _ _    _ _ _ _ _

   _ _ _ _    _ _ _ _ _    _ _ _ _    _ _ _ _ _


2. make        makes        5. live        lived
   make        make__              live        live__

   _ _ _ _    _ _ _ _ _    _ _ _ _    _ _ _ _

   _ _ _ _    _ _ _ _ _    _ _ _ _    _ _ _ _


3. state        states        6. right        rights
   state        state__              right        right__

   _ _ _ _ _    _ _ _ _ _ _    _ _ _ _ _    _ _ _ _ _ _

   _ _ _ _ _    _ _ _ _ _ _    _ _ _ _ _    _ _ _ _ _ _

**CD 2 TRACK 8** **Listen/Look. Listen/Say. Copy. Listen/Say.**

1. We want to come.

_____ _____ _____ _____.

2. They make laws.

_____ _____ _____.

3. We have rights.

_____ _____ _____.

4. The stripes are red and white.

_____ _____ _____ _____ _____.

 **CD 2 TRACK 9** **Read-alouds**

1. Who is George?

2. How do we vote?

3. When is Flag Day?

4. Where is New York?

5. Why do we have laws?

6. Who lives in the White House?

TEACHER    *Top:* Follow instructions, p. 12, bottom.  *Bottom:* Follow instructions, p. 43, bottom.

**CD 2 TRACK 10**  **Listen. Write.**

1. _____ _____ _____ .

2. _____ _____ _____ .

3. _____ _____ _____ _____ .

4. _____ _____ _____ _____ _____ _____ .

**CD 2 TRACK 11**  **Read-alouds**

1. Why do they come here?

2. Why do they want to vote?

3. Where is the White House?

4. Where can we meet George?

5. What is the Bill of Rights?

6. Who lived here first?

*Bill of Rights*

TEACHER  *Top:* Dictation: 1. They make laws.  2. We have rights.  3. We want to come.  4. The stripes are red and white.  *Bottom:* Follow instructions, p. 43, bottom.

# 9.

dollar

people

Lincoln

city

during

country

second

Congress

TEACHER   Follow instructions for word cards in the *Teacher's Guide*, p. 45.

Section 9   57

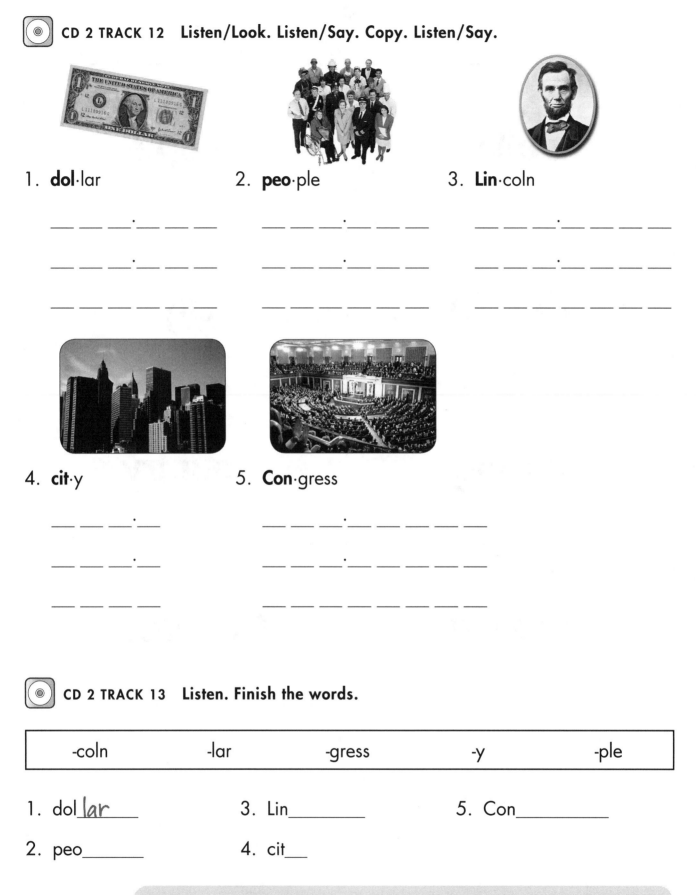

CD 2 TRACK 12    Listen/Look. Listen/Say. Copy. Listen/Say.

1. **dol**·lar

2. **peo**·ple

3. **Lin**·coln

4. **cit**·y

5. **Con**·gress

CD 2 TRACK 13    Listen. Finish the words.

| -coln | -lar | -gress | -y | -ple |
| --- | --- | --- | --- | --- |

1. dol _lar_

2. peo_____

3. Lin_____

4. cit___

5. Con_____

TEACHER    *Top:* Follow instructions, p. 9, top. Voice each syllable distinctly. *Bottom:* Point to and read the first word. Have students find the ending of the word in the box. Use the model to show how to complete each word. Point to and read the other words, and have students complete them.

**Match.**

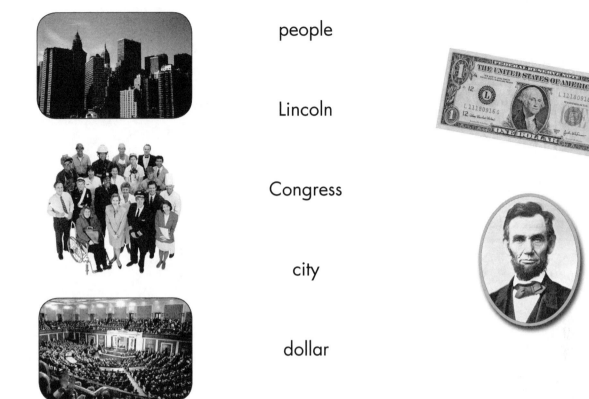

people

Lincoln

Congress

city

dollar

 **CD 2 TRACK 14   Listen/Look. Listen/Say. Copy. Listen/Say.**

1. **wash**·ing

2. **giv**·ing

3. **dur**·ing

\_ \_ \_ \_ · \_ \_ \_          \_ \_ \_ · \_ \_ \_          \_ \_ \_ · \_ \_ \_

\_ \_ \_ \_ · \_ \_ \_          \_ \_ \_ · \_ \_ \_          \_ \_ \_ · \_ \_ \_

\_ \_ \_ \_ \_ \_ \_          \_ \_ \_ \_ \_ \_          \_ \_ \_ \_ \_ \_

TEACHER   *Top:* Follow instructions, p. 31, top. *Bottom:* Follow instructions, p. 9, top. Voice each syllable distinctly.

Section 9   **59**

**CD 2 TRACK 15    Listen. Look. Say.**

1. How

2. many

3. How many

4. What

5. Where

6. When

7. Why

**CD 2 TRACK 16    Listen. Write the letters.**

| -ing |
|------|

1. wash___ ___ ___

2. giv___ ___ ___

3. dur___ ___ ___

| -y |
|----|

4. cit___

5. man___

6. countr___

7. Februar___

**CD 2 TRACK 17    Listen. Finish the words.**

| Con-     cit-     Lin-     peo-     dol- |
|------|

1. _____ple

2. _____gress

3. _____coln

4. _____lar

5. _____y

TEACHER    *Top:* Follow instructions, p. 51, center. (Note: It is important for students to distinguish between these words, as most citizenship test reading items ("read aloud" questions) begin with them.) *Center:* Point to the letters *–ing* and pronounce the sound they make. Read each word and have students fill in the missing *–ing.* Do the same with the *–y* words. *Bottom:* Point to and read the first word. Have students find the beginning of the word in the box and copy it on the line. Do the same with each word.

**Write the word to match the picture. Use words in the box.**

| Lincoln | dollar | washing | Congress | giving | people | city |
|---------|--------|---------|----------|--------|--------|------|

1. _ _ _ _

2. _ _ _ _ _ _

3. _ _ _ _ _ _ _

4. _ _ _ _ _ _

5. _ _ _ _ _ _

6. _ _ _ _ _ _ _

7. _ _ _ _ _ _ _ _

---

CD 2 TRACK 18  **Listen/Look. Listen/Say. Copy. Listen/Say.**

1. **sec**·ond

_ _ _·_ _

_ _ _·_ _

_ _ _·_ _

2. **coun**·try

_ _ _ _·_ _

_ _ _ _·_ _

_ _ _ _·_ _

3. **dur**·ing

_ _ _·_ _

_ _ _·_ _

_ _ _·_ _

**CD 2 TRACK 19   Listen. Finish the words.**

| -ing | -ond | -try |
|------|------|------|

1. sec_____      2. coun_____      3. dur_____

**Circle: Who is second?**

**Circle the country.**

**How <u>many</u>?**

1       __       __       __

**Circle: Which <u>country</u> do we live in?**

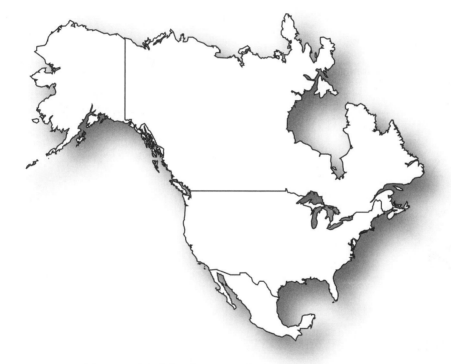

🔘 **CD 2 TRACK 20**   **Listen. Finish the words.**

| sec- | coun- | dur- |
|------|-------|------|

1. _____ing     2. _____ond     3. _____try

TEACHER   *Top:* Have students read the question and write the correct number on each line. *Center:* Have students read the question and circle the outline of the U.S. on the map. *Bottom:* Follow instructions, p. 58, bottom.

1. **dol**lar **bill**

_____ bill

dollar _____

_____ _____

_____ _____

2. New York **Cit**y

_____ York City

New _____ City

_____ York _____

_____ _____ _____

3. **fa**ther of our **coun**try

_____ of our country

father _____ _____ country

_____ of _____ country

_____ _____ _____ _____

TEACHER   Point to each phrase and have students listen as you say it. Help students read the phrase aloud, then copy the words onto the blanks.

**64**   Section 9

**How <u>many</u> people?**

\_\_\_          \_\_\_          \_\_\_                    \_\_\_

**How <u>many</u> stripes?**

\_\_\_          \_\_\_          \_\_\_          \_\_\_

---

CD 2 TRACK 22   **Listen. Write.**

1. _____          2. _____          3. _____          4. _____

---

CD 2 TRACK 23   **Listen/Look. Listen/Say. Copy. Listen/Say.**

1. Lincoln lived in the North.

   _____ _____ \_\_\_\_ \_\_\_\_\_ _____.

2. New York is a city.

   _____ _____ \_\_\_\_ \_\_ _____.

3. Congress meets here.

   _____ _____ _____.

TEACHER   *Top:* Have students read the questions and write the correct number on each line.
*Center: Spelling quiz:* 1. dollar  2. people  3. Lincoln  4. city. *Bottom:* Follow instructions,
p. 12, bottom.

**CD 2 TRACK 24**   **Listen. Write.**

1. _____   2. _____   3. _____   4. _____

**CD 2 TRACK 25**   **Listen/Look. Listen/Say. Copy. Listen/Say.**

1. They lived here during the war.

   _____ _____ _____ _____ _____.

2. He is the father of our country.

   ____ ____ ____ _____ ____ _____.

3. They live in the second house.

   _____ ____ ____ _____ _____.

4. They want a dollar.

   _____ _____ __ _____.

**CD 2 TRACK 26**   **Listen. Write.**

1. ____ ____ ____ _____ ____ ____ _____.

2. _____ _____ _____ _____ _____.

3. _____ ____ _____.

TEACHER   *Top: Spelling quiz:* 1. during  2. country  3. second  4. Congress. *Center:* Follow instructions, p. 12, bottom. *Bottom: Dictation:* 1. He is the father of our country.  2. They lived here during the war.  3. Congress meets here.

**CD 2 TRACK 27   Read-alouds**

1. Who is the Father of our Country?

2. Where does Congress meet?

3. Who is on the dollar bill?

4. Where was George during the war?

5. What state has the most people?

6. How many people live here?

7. How many states does our country have?

 **CD 2 TRACK 28   Listen. Write.**

1. _____ _____ _____ _____ _____.

2. _____ _____ _____ _____ _____ _____.

3. _____ _____ _____ ____ _____.

4. _____ _____ ____ _____.

TEACHER   *Top:* Follow instructions, p. 43, bottom.  ***Bottom: Dictation:*** 1. Lincoln lived in the North.  2. They live in the second house.  3. New York is a city.  4. They want a dollar.

# 10.

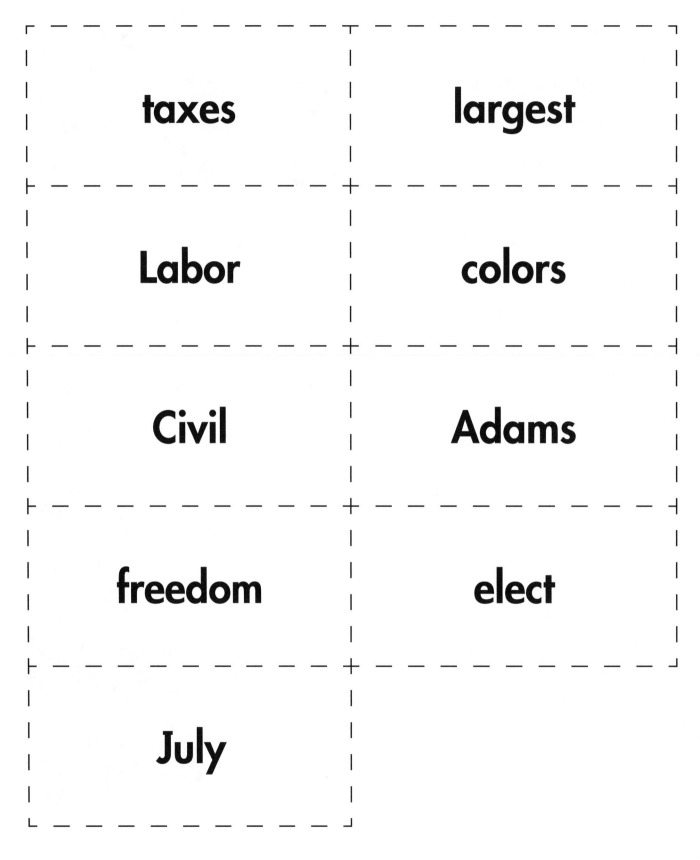

taxes

largest

Labor

colors

Civil

Adams

freedom

elect

July

TEACHER   Follow instructions for word cards in the *Teacher's Guide,* p. 45.

**68**   Section 10

1. **tax**·es

— — — — . — — — —

— — — — . — — — —

— — — — . — — — —

2. **col**·ors

— — — — . — — — —

— — — — . — — — —

— — — — . — — — —

3. **La**·bor

— — — . — — — —

— — — . — — — —

— — — . — — — —

4. **Civ**·il

— — — . — — —

— — — . — — —

— — — . — — —

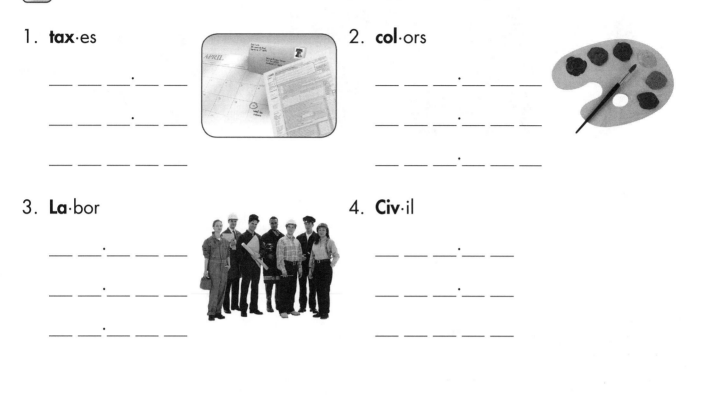

⊚ CD 2 TRACK 30  Listen. Finish the words.

| -bor | -il | -ors | -es |
|---|---|---|---|

1. tax _____  2. La _____  3. col _____  4. Civ_____

**Circle: Who pays <u>taxes</u>?**

TEACHER  *Top:* Follow directions, p. 9, top. Voice each syllable distinctly. *Center:* Follow instructions, p. 58, bottom. *Bottom:* Have students read the question and circle the appropriate response.

**Circle: What do our <u>taxes</u> pay for?**

**Circle the <u>colors</u>.**

for          red          is          white          are          bill          blue

CD 2 TRACK 31    **Listen. Finish the words.**

| col- | Civ- | tax- | La- |

1. _____bor          2. _____il          3. _____ors          4. _____es

TEACHER    *Top:* Have students read the question and discuss each of the pictures (military, schools, etc.). Point out that all of them are paid for by taxes, so that students understand that all the answers are correct. *Bottom:* Follow instructions, p. 58, bottom.

**CD 2 TRACK 32** **Listen/Look. Listen/Say. Copy. Listen/Say.**

1. **Ad**·ams

2. **free**·dom

3. **larg**·est

___ ___ · ___ ___ ___     ___ ___ ___ ___ · ___ ___     ___ ___ ___ · ___ ___ ___ ___

___ ___ · ___ ___ ___     ___ ___ ___ ___ · ___ ___     ___ ___ ___ · ___ ___ ___ ___

___ ___ ___ ___     ___ ___ ___ ___ ___ ___     ___ ___ ___ ___ ___ ___ ___

**Circle: Which state is the <u>largest</u>?**

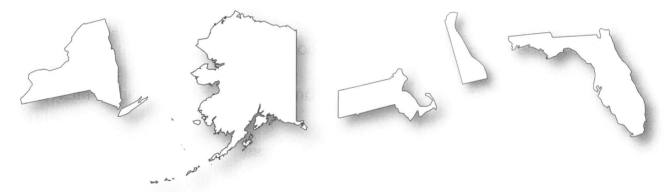

**Circle: What is <u>freedom</u>?**

TEACHER   *Top:* Follow instructions, p. 9, top. Voice each syllable distinctly. *Bottom:* Have students read the questions and circle the correct response to each.

Section 10   **71**

**Circle: Who was the <u>second</u> president?**

1. Washington (1789)     2. Adams (1797)     3. Jefferson (1801)

 **CD 2 TRACK 33   Listen/Look. Listen/Say. Copy. Listen/Say.**

    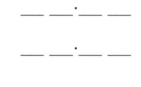

1. e·**lect**

__·__ __ __ __

__·__ __ __ __

__ __ __ __ __

2. Ju·**ly**

__ __·__ __

__ __·__ __

__ __ __ __

 **CD 2 TRACK 34   Listen. Finish the words.**

| -dom | -ly | -lect | -ams | -gest |
|------|-----|-------|------|-------|

1. Ad_____     3. free_____     5. Ju_____

2. e_____      4. lar_____

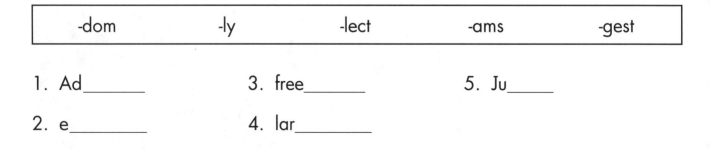
TEACHER   *Top:* Have students read the question and circle the correct answer (Adams).
*Center:* Follow instructions, p. 9, top. Voice each syllable distinctly.  *Bottom:* Follow instructions,
p. 58, bottom.

**CD 2 TRACK 35**  **Listen. Say. Copy on the lines.**

1. **La**bor Day

_____ Day

Labor _____

_____ _____

_____ _____

2. Civil **War**

_____ War

Civil _____

_____ _____

_____ _____

3. **free**dom of **speech**

_____ of speech

freedom of _____

_____ _____ speech

_____ _____ _____

TEACHER   Follow instructions, p. 64.

🔘 **CD 2 TRACK 36   Listen. Finish the words.**

| free- | lar- | Ad- | Ju- | e- |
|---|---|---|---|---|

1. _____ams          3. __lect          5. _____ly

2. _____dom          4. _____gest


🔘 **CD 2 TRACK 37   Listen. Write.**

1. _____          2. _____          3. _____          4. _____


🔘 **CD 2 TRACK 38   Listen/Look. Listen/Say. Copy. Listen/Say.**

1. Labor Day is in September.

_____ _____ _____ _____ _____.


2. We have freedom of speech.

_____ _____ _____ _____ _____.


3. They lived during the Civil War.

_____ _____ _____ _____ _____ _____.


4. We pay taxes.

_____ _____ _____.

5. Independence Day is in July.

_____ _____ _____ ____ _____ .

CD 2 TRACK 39   **Listen. Write.**

1. _____      3. _____      5. _____

2. _____      4. _____

CD 2 TRACK 40   **Listen/Look. Listen/Say. Copy. Listen/Say.**

1. Alaska is the largest state.

_____ _____ _____ _____ _____ .

2. The colors of the flag are red, white, and blue.

_____ _____ ____ ____ _____ _____

_____ , _____ , _____ _____ .

3. The people elect Congress.

_____ _____ _____ .

4. Adams was the second president.

_____ _____ _____ _____ _____ .

---

TEACHER   *Top:* Continue from p. 74. *Center: Spelling quiz:* 1. civil  2. Adams  3. freedom
4. elect  5. July. *Bottom:* Follow instructions, p. 12, bottom.

**CD 2 TRACK 41   Listen. Write.**

1. _____ _____ _____ _____ September.

2. _____ _____ _____ _____ _____.

3. _____ _____ _____ _____

   _____ _____.

4. _____ _____ _____.

5. Independence _____ _____ _____ _____.

**CD 2 TRACK 42   Read-alouds**

1. When is Labor Day?

2. Who has freedom of speech?

3. What was the Civil War?

4. Why do we pay taxes?

**CD 2 TRACK 43  Listen. Write.**

1. Alaska _____ _____ _____ _____.

2. _____ _____ ____ ____ _____ _____

_____ _____, _____, _____ _____.

3. _____ _____ _____ _____.

4. _____ _____ _____ _____ president.

**CD 2 TRACK 44  Read-alouds**

1. Who elects Congress?

2. What is the largest state?

3. What are the colors of the flag?

TEACHER  *Top: Dictation:* 1. Alaska is the largest state.  2. The colors of the flag are red, white, and blue.  3. The people elect Congress.  4. Adams was the second president.
*Bottom:* Follow instructions, p. 43, bottom.

# 11.

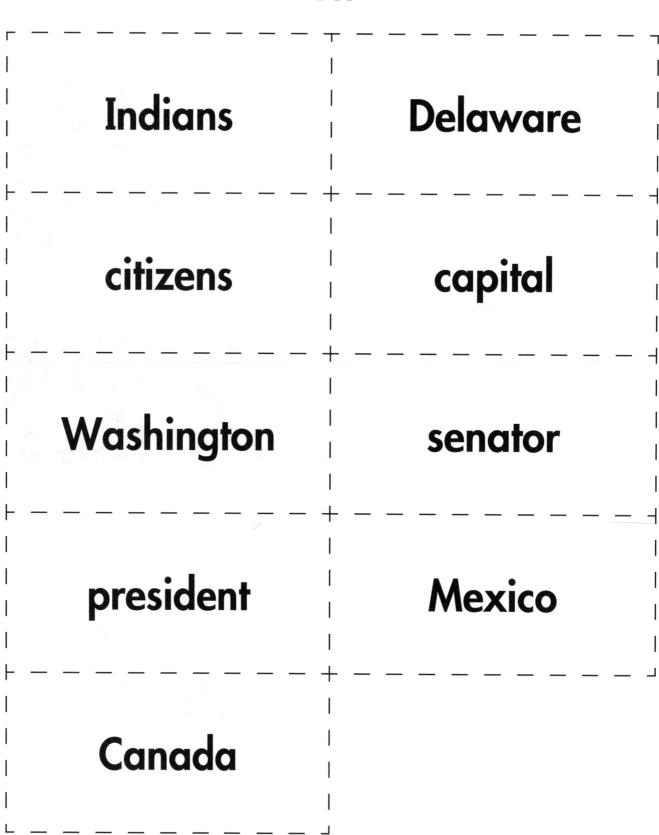

| Indians | Delaware |
| citizens | capital |
| Washington | senator |
| president | Mexico |
| Canada | |

TEACHER   Follow instructions for word cards in the *Teacher's Guide*, p. 45.

**78**   Section 11

1. **Wash**·ing·ton          2. **cit**·i·zens          3. **Del**·a·ware

_____ . ____ . ____          _____ . ____ . ____          _____ . __ . __

_____ . ____ . ____          _____ . ____ . ____          _____ . __ . __

_____ ____ ____          _____ ____ ____          _____ __ __

## Circle: Which state was <u>first</u>?

Delaware          New York          North Carolina

## Circle: Where is <u>George Washington</u>?

**TEACHER**   *Top:* Follow instructions, p. 9, top. Voice each syllable distinctly. *Bottom:* Have students read each question and circle the appropriate answers. Have them look at the dates to understand which state was first.

**Circle: Where is <u>Abraham Lincoln</u>?**

 **CD 2 TRACK 46**    Listen/Look. Listen/Say. Copy. Listen/Say.

1. **In**·di·ans          2. **Mex**·i·co          3. **Can**·a·da

_____ . _____ . _____          _____ . _____ . _____          _____ . _____ . _____

_____ . _____ . _____          _____ . _____ . _____          _____ . _____ . _____

_____ . _____ . _____          _____ . _____ . _____          _____ . _____ . _____

**Circle the <u>Indians</u>:**

Circle <u>Mexico</u>. Write the name.

Circle <u>Canada</u>. Write the name.

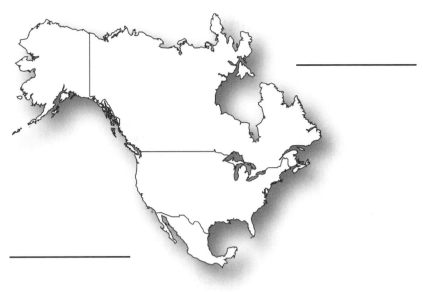

_____

_____

CD 2 TRACK 47 Listen/Look. Listen/Say. Copy. Listen/Say.

1. **cap**·i·tal

2. **pres**·i·dent

3. **sen**·a·tors

_____ . _____ . _____          _____ . _____ . _____          _____ . _____ . _____

_____ . _____ . _____          _____ . _____ . _____          _____ . _____ . _____

_____ ___ _____          _____ ___ _____          _____ . _____ . _____

Circle the U.S. <u>capital</u>.

New York City

Washington, D.C.

TEACHER   *Top:* Have students read the instructions, circle the countries indicated, and write the names of the countries on the appropriate blanks. *Center:* Follow instructions, p. 9, top. Voice each syllable distinctly. *Bottom:* Have students read the underlined word and circle the correct picture.

**Circle: Who was the first <u>president</u>?**

Washington

Lincoln

Adams

**Circle: How many <u>senators</u> are in the U.S. Congress?**

3              50              100

 **CD 2 TRACK 48    Listen/Look. Listen/Say.**

1. **gov**·ern·ment              government

2. **A**·bra·ham              Abraham

3. **A**·bra·ham **Lin**·coln              Abraham Lincoln

4. **Wash**·ing·ton              Washington

5. George **Wash**·ing·ton              George Washington

6. **Wash**·ing·ton, D.C.              Washington, D.C.

7. **pres**·i·dents              presidents

8. **Pres**·i·dents' Day              Presidents' Day

| FEBRUARY | | | | | | |
|---|---|---|---|---|---|---|
| S | M | T | W | T | F | S |
|  | 1 | 2 | 3 | 4 | 5 | 6 |
| 7 | 8 | 9 | 10 | 11 | 12 | 13 |
| 14 | 15 | 16 | 17 | 18 | 19 | 20 |
| 21 | 22 | 23 | 24 | 25 | 26 | 27 |
| 28 |  |  |  |  |  |  |

TEACHER    *Top:* Have students read the questions and circle the appropriate answers.
*Bottom:* Point to and read each word twice, first voicing each syllable distinctly, then reading the word normally. Do this again and have students repeat. Then have students read each word to you.

**Match.**

George Washington

Abraham Lincoln

Mexico

Canada

Indians

 **CD 2 TRACK 49   Listen. Say. Copy on the lines.**

| FEBRUARY | | | | | | |
|---|---|---|---|---|---|---|
| S | M | T | W | T | F | S |
|  | 1 | 2 | 3 | 4 | 5 | 6 |
| 7 | 8 | 9 | 10 | 11 | 12 | 13 |
| 14 | 15 | 16 | 17 | 18 | 19 | 20 |
| 21 | 22 | 23 | 24 | 25 | 26 | 27 |
| 28 |  |  |  |  |  |  |

1. **Pres**idents' Day

   _____idents' Day

   Pres\_\_\_\_dents' _____

   _____i_____ Day

   _____ _____

2. **Wash**ington, D.C.

   Wash_____, D.C.

   _____ington, \_\_.\_\_.

   Washing_____, \_\_.\_\_.

   _____, \_\_.\_\_.

TEACHER   *Top:* Follow instructions, p. 31, top. *Bottom:* Follow instructions, p. 64.

Section 11   **83**

**Write the word to match the picture. Use words in the box.**

| Canada | Washington | Indians | Mexico |
|--------|-----------|---------|--------|

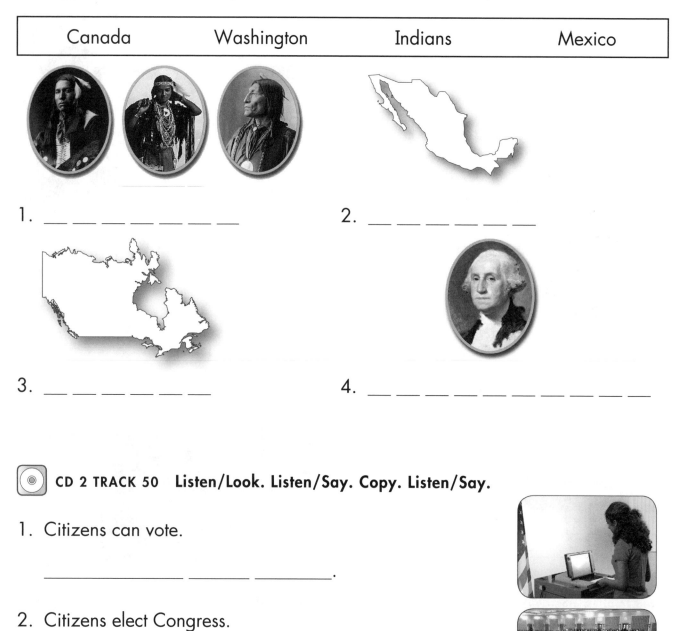

1. __ __ __ __ __ __ __

2. __ __ __ __ __ __

3. __ __ __ __ __ __

4. __ __ __ __ __ __ __ __ __ __

CD 2 TRACK 50   **Listen/Look. Listen/Say. Copy. Listen/Say.**

1. Citizens can vote.

   _____ _____ _____.

2. Citizens elect Congress.

   _____ _____ _____.

3. Mexico is south of the U.S.

   _____ _____ _____ _____ _____ __.__.

TEACHER   *Top:* Follow instructions, p. 61, top. ***Bottom:*** Follow instructions, p. 12, bottom. Exercise continues on p. 85.

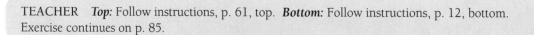

4. Canada is north of the U.S.

_____ _____ _____ _____ _____ ___.___.

5. Lincoln was president during the Civil War.

_____ _____ _____ _____

_____ _____ _____.

6. Washington was the first president.

_____ _____ _____ _____ _____.

7. Congress has 100 senators.

_____ _____ _____ _____.

🔘 **CD 2 TRACK 51   Read-alouds.**

1. Who was the first president?

2. What president is on the dollar bill?

3. When do we vote for president?

4. What is the capital of the U.S.?

| NOVEMBER | | | | | | |
|---|---|---|---|---|---|---|
| S | M | T | W | T | F | S |
| | 1 | 2 | 3 | 4 | 5 | 6 |
| 7 | 8 | 9 | 10 | 11 | 12 | 13 |
| 14 | 15 | 16 | 17 | 18 | 19 | 20 |
| 21 | 22 | 23 | 24 | 25 | 26 | 27 |
| 28 | 29 | 30 | | | | |

TEACHER   *Top:* Continue from p. 84. ***Bottom:*** Follow instructions, p. 43, bottom.

◎ **CD 2 TRACK 52   Listen. Write.**

1. _____ _____ _____.

2. _____ _____ _____.

3. _____ _____ _____ _____ ___.___.

4. _____ _____ _____ _____ ___.___.

5. _____ _____ _____

   _____ _____ _____.

6. _____ _____ _____

   _____ _____.

7. _____ _____ _____.

◎ **CD 2 TRACK 53   Listen/Look. Listen/Say. Copy. Listen/Say.**

1. Delaware was the first state.

   _____ _____ _____ _____ _____.

2. The president lives in the White House.

   _____ _____ _____ _____

   _____ _____ _____.

3. The White House is in Washington, D.C.

   _____ _____ _____ _____ _____

   _____, ___.___.

> TEACHER   *Top:* Dictation: 1. Citizens can vote.  2. Citizens elect Congress.  3. Mexico is south of the U.S.  4. Canada is north of the U.S.  5. Lincoln was president during the Civil War. 6. Washington was the first president.  7. Congress has 100 senators. ***Bottom:*** Follow instructions, p. 12, bottom. Exercise continues on p. 87.

4. Congress meets in Washington, D.C.

_____ _____ _____

_____, __.__.

5. Washington, D.C. is the capital of the U.S.

_____, __.__. _____ _____

_____ _____ _____ __.__.

6. New York City was the first capital.

_____ _____ _____ _____ _____

_____ _____.

◎ **CD 2 TRACK 54**   **Listen. Write.**

1. _____    3. _____    5. _____

2. _____    4. _____

◎ **CD 2 TRACK 55**   **Read-alouds.**

1. What country is north of the U.S.?

2. What country is south of the U.S.?

3. When is Presidents' Day?

4. How many senators are in Congress?

5. Why do people want to be citizens?

TEACHER   *Top:* Continue from p. 86. *Center: Spelling quiz:* 1. Mexico  2. Canada  3. senator
4. capital  5. Indians. *Bottom:* Follow instructions, p. 43, bottom.

1. _____ _____ _____ _____ _____.

2. _____ _____ _____ ____
   _____ _____ _____.

3. _____ _____ _____ _____ ____
   _____, ___.___.

4. _____ _____ _____
   _____, ___.___.

5. _____, ___.___. _____ _____ _____
   _____ _____ _____ ___.___.

6. _____ _____ _____ _____
   _____ _____.

1. Who was the second president?

2. Who was George Washington?

3. What do we pay to the government?

4. What was the first capital of the U.S.?

5. Who was Abraham Lincoln?

TEACHER   *Top: Dictation:* 1. Delaware was the first state.  2. The president lives in the White House.  3. The White House is in Washington, D.C.  4. Congress meets in Washington, D.C.  5. Washington, D.C. is the capital of the U.S.  6. New York City was the first capital.
*Bottom:* Follow instructions, p. 43, bottom.

# 12.

Columbus

Alaska

United

September

October

November

Thanksgiving

TEACHER   Follow instructions for word cards in the *Teacher's Guide,* p. 45.

Section 12   **89**

1. Co·**lum**·bus         2. A·**las**·ka         3. U·**ni**·ted

\_\_\_\_\_ · \_\_\_\_\_ · \_\_\_\_\_     \_\_\_\_ · \_\_\_\_\_ · \_\_\_\_\_     \_\_\_ · \_\_\_\_\_ · \_\_\_\_

\_\_\_\_\_ · \_\_\_\_\_ · \_\_\_\_\_     \_\_\_\_ · \_\_\_\_\_ · \_\_\_\_\_     \_\_\_ · \_\_\_\_\_ · \_\_\_\_

\_\_\_\_\_ \_\_\_\_\_ \_\_\_\_\_     \_\_\_\_ \_\_\_\_\_ \_\_\_\_\_     \_\_\_ \_\_\_\_\_ \_\_\_\_

**Circle: What state is the <u>largest</u>?**

Delaware          New York          Washington          Alaska

TEACHER   *Top:* Follow instructions, p. 9, top. Voice each syllable distinctly. ***Bottom:*** Have students read the question and circle the appropriate answer.

1. Co·**lum**·bus Day

   _____lumbus Day

   Co_____bus _____

   _____lum_____ Day

   _____ _____

2. U·**ni**·ted **States**

   __nited _____

   U_____ted States

   Uni_____ _____

   _____ _____

**CD 2 TRACK 60**  **Listen/Look. Listen/Say. Copy. Listen/Say.**

1. Sep·**tem**·ber

   _____·_____·_____

   _____·_____·_____

   _____ _____

2. Oc·**to**·ber

   _____·_____·_____

   _____·_____·_____

   _____ _____

3. No·**vem**·ber

   _____·_____·_____

   _____·_____·_____

   _____ _____

4. Thanks·**giv**·ing

   _____·_____·_____

   _____·_____·_____

   _____ _____

TEACHER   *Top:* Follow instructions, p. 64.  *Bottom:* Follow instructions, p. 9, top. Voice each syllable distinctly.

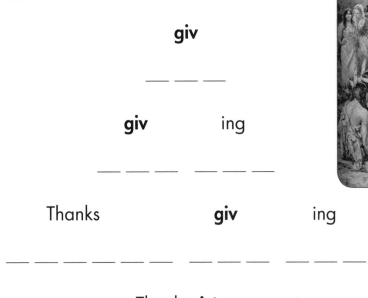

**CD 2 TRACK 61**   **Listen. Copy.**

**giv**

— — —

**giv**        ing

— — —   — — —

Thanks        **giv**        ing

— — — — —   — — — — —   — — —

Thanks**giv**ing

— — — — — — — — — — — — —

**CD 2 TRACK 62**   **Listen/Look. Listen/Say. Copy. Listen/Say.**

1. Columbus Day is in October.

_____ _____ ___ ___ _____.

2. We vote in November.

_____ _____ __ _____.

3. Labor Day is in September.

_____ ___ __ __ _____.

4. Alaska is the largest state.

_____ ___ ___ _____ _____.

TEACHER   *Top:* Point to and read each syllable/word while students listen. Have students copy the syllables/words onto the blanks. Read again and have students repeat. Then have students read the syllables/words to you. *Bottom:* Follow instructions, p. 12, bottom.

| SEPTEMBER | | | | | | |
|---|---|---|---|---|---|---|
| S | M | T | W | T | F | S |
| | 1 | 2 | 3 | 4 | 5 | 6 |
| 7 | 8 | 9 | 10 | 11 | 12 | 13 |
| 14 | 15 | 16 | 17 | 18 | 19 | 20 |
| 21 | 22 | 23 | 25 | 26 | 27 | 28 |
| 29 | 30 | | | | | |

| OCTOBER | | | | | | |
|---|---|---|---|---|---|---|
| S | M | T | W | T | F | S |
| | | | | | 1 | 2 |
| 3 | 4 | 5 | 6 | 7 | 8 | 9 |
| 10 | 11 | 12 | 13 | 14 | 15 | 16 |
| 17 | 18 | 19 | 20 | 21 | 22 | 23 |
| 24/31 | 25 | 26 | 27 | 28 | 29 | 30 |

| NOVEMBER | | | | | | |
|---|---|---|---|---|---|---|
| S | M | T | W | T | F | S |
| | 1 | 2 | 3 | 4 | 5 | 6 |
| 7 | 8 | 9 | 10 | 11 | 12 | 13 |
| 14 | 15 | 16 | 17 | 18 | 19 | 20 |
| 21 | 22 | 23 | 24 | 25 | 26 | 27 |
| 28 | 29 | 30 | | | | |

**Circle: When is <u>Columbus Day</u>?**

September          October          November

**Circle: When is <u>Labor Day</u>?**

September          October          November

**Circle: When is <u>Thanksgiving</u>?**

September          October          November

**Circle: When do we vote for president?**

September          October          November

 **CD 2 TRACK 63    Listen. Write.**

1. _____          3. _____

2. _____          4. _____

**CD 2 TRACK 64**   **Listen/Look. Listen/Say. Copy. Listen/Say.**

1. The United States has 50 states.

   _____ _____ _____ \_\_\_\_\_ \_\_\_\_\_ _____.

2. We elect the president in November.

   \_\_\_\_\_ _____ \_\_\_\_\_ _____

   \_\_\_\_\_ _____.

3. Thanksgiving is in November.

   _____ \_\_\_\_\_ \_\_\_\_\_ _____.

**CD 2 TRACK 65**   **Listen. Write.**

1. _____        3. _____

2. _____

**CD 2 TRACK 66**   **Listen. Write.**

1. _____ _____ \_\_\_\_ \_\_\_\_ _____.

2. \_\_\_\_\_ _____ \_\_\_\_ _____.

3. _____ _____ \_\_\_\_ _____.

4. _____ \_\_\_\_ \_\_\_\_ _____.

TEACHER   *Top:* Follow instructions, p. 12, bottom.   ***Center:*** *Spelling quiz:* 1. October
2. November   3. Thanksgiving.   ***Bottom:*** *Dictation:* 1. Columbus Day is in October.   2. We vote
in November.   3. Labor Day is in September.   4. Alaska is the largest state.

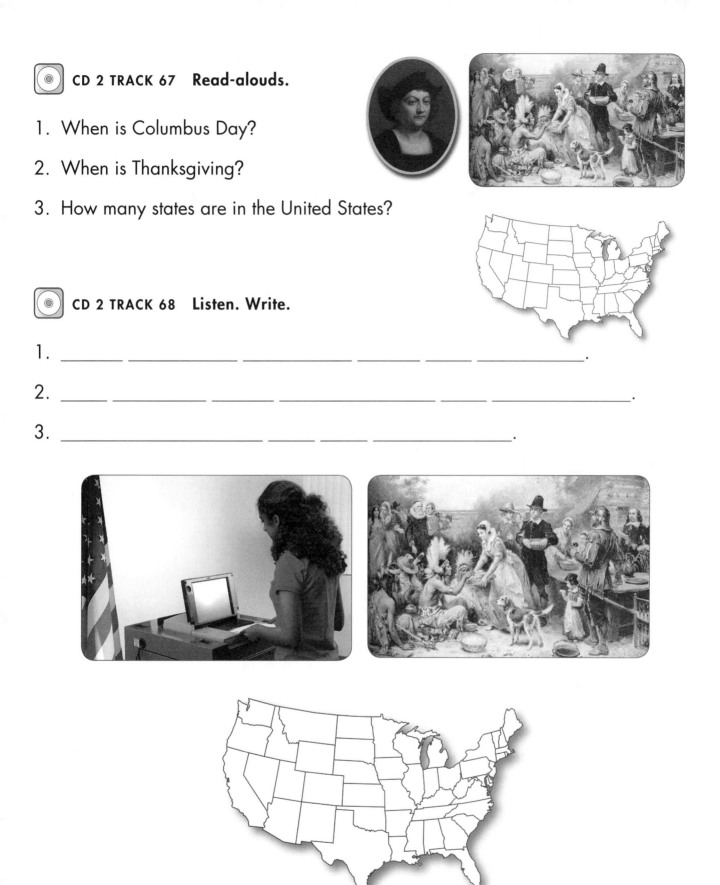

💿 **CD 2 TRACK 67**  **Read-alouds.**

1. When is Columbus Day?

2. When is Thanksgiving?

3. How many states are in the United States?

💿 **CD 2 TRACK 68**  **Listen. Write.**

1. _____ _____ _____ _____ _____ _____.

2. _____ _____ _____ _____ ____ _____.

3. _____ _____ _____ _____.

TEACHER   *Top:* Follow instructions, p. 43, bottom.  **Bottom:** *Dictation:* 1. The United States has 50 states.  2. We elect the president in November.  3. Thanksgiving is in November.

# 13.

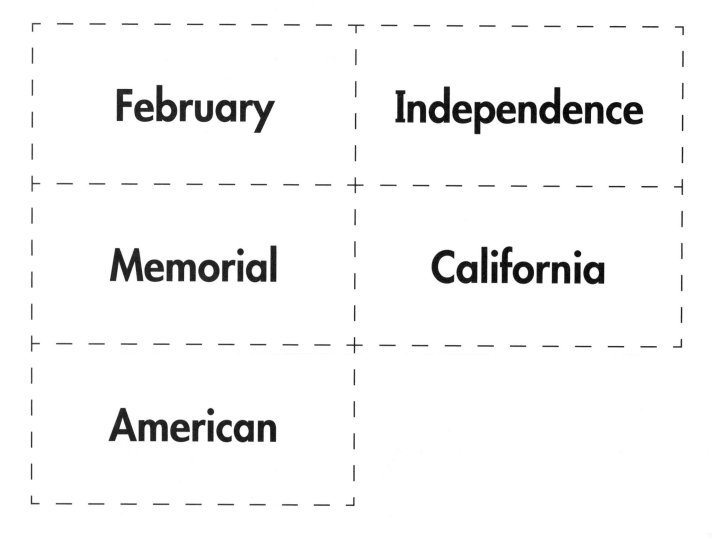

February

Independence

Memorial

California

American

TEACHER   Follow instructions for word cards in the *Teacher's Guide*, p. 45.

**96**   Section 13

**CD 2 TRACK 69  Listen/Look. Listen/Say. Copy. Listen/Say.**

| FEBRUARY | | | | | | |
|---|---|---|---|---|---|---|
| S | M | T | W | T | F | S |
| | 1 | 2 | 3 | 4 | 5 | 6 |
| 7 | 8 | 9 | 10 | 11 | 12 | 13 |
| 14 | 15 | 16 | 17 | 18 | 19 | 20 |
| 21 | 22 | 23 | 24 | 25 | 26 | 27 |
| 28 | | | | | | |

1. **Feb**·ru·ar·y

2. Mem·**or**·i·al

_____ · _____ · _____ · __        _____ · _____ · _ · ____

_____ · _____ · _____ · __        _____ · _____ · _ · ____

_____ · _____ · _____          _____ __ _____ __ ____

3. In·de·**pen**·dence

_____ · ____ · _____ · _____

_____ · ____ · _____ · _____

_____ __ _____ __ _____

TEACHER   Follow instructions, p. 9, top. Voice each syllable distinctly.

| | | FEBRUARY | | | | |
|---|---|---|---|---|---|---|
| S | M | T | W | T | F | S |
| | 1 | 2 | 3 | 4 | 5 | 6 |
| 7 | 8 | 9 | 10 | 11 | 12 | 13 |
| 14 | 15 | 16 | 17 | 18 | 19 | 20 |
| 21 | 22 | 23 | 24 | 25 | 26 | 27 |
| 28 | | | | | | |

| | | | MAY | | | |
|---|---|---|---|---|---|---|
| S | M | T | W | T | F | S |
| 1 | 2 | 3 | 4 | 5 | 6 | 7 |
| 8 | 9 | 10 | 11 | 12 | 13 | 14 |
| 15 | 16 | 17 | 18 | 19 | 20 | 21 |
| 22 | 23 | 24 | 25 | 26 | 27 | 28 |
| 29 | 30 | 31 | | | | |

| | | | JULY | | | |
|---|---|---|---|---|---|---|
| S | M | T | W | T | F | S |
| | | | | 1 | 2 | 3 |
| 4 | 5 | 6 | 7 | 8 | 9 | 10 |
| 11 | 12 | 13 | 14 | 15 | 16 | 17 |
| 18 | 19 | 20 | 21 | 22 | 23 | 24 |
| 25 | 26 | 27 | 28 | 29 | 30 | 31 |

## Circle: When is <u>Memorial Day</u>?

February             May             July

## Circle: When is <u>Independence Day</u>?

February             May             July

## Circle: When is <u>Presidents' Day</u>?

February             May             July

TEACHER   Have students read each question and circle the appropriate month.

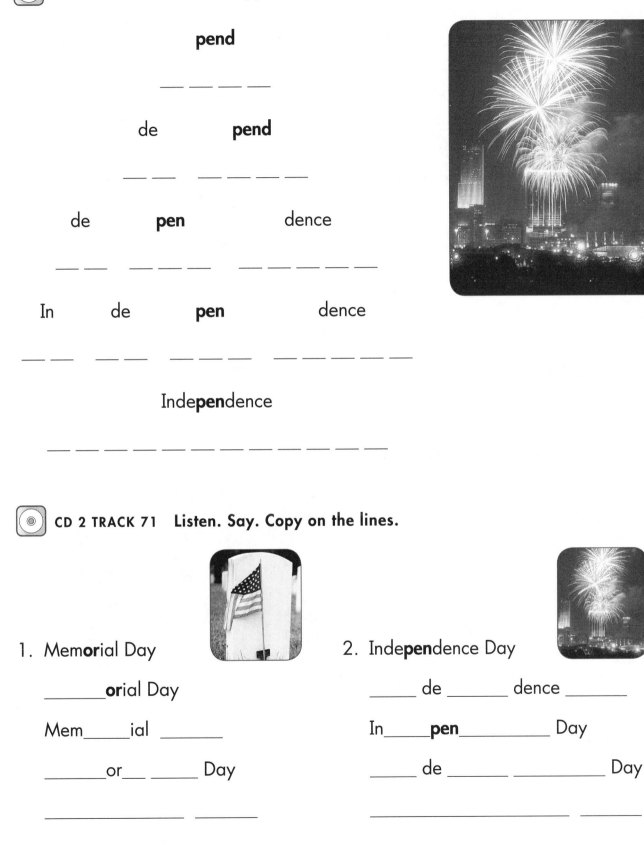

**CD 2 TRACK 70** **Listen. Copy.**

**pend**

— — — —

de      **pend**

— — — — — —

de      **pen**      dence

— — — — — — — —

In    de    **pen**    dence

— — — — — — — —

Inde**pen**dence

— — — — — — — — — — —

**CD 2 TRACK 71** **Listen. Say. Copy on the lines.**

1. Mem**o**rial Day

_____**or**ial Day

Mem\_\_\_\_\_ial _____

_____or\_\_ \_\_\_\_\_ Day

_____ _____

2. Inde**pen**dence Day

\_\_\_\_ de _____ dence _____

In\_\_\_\_\_**pen**_____ Day

\_\_\_\_ de _____ _____ Day

_____ \_\_\_\_\_

TEACHER    *Top:* Follow instructions, p. 92, top.   *Bottom:* Follow instructions, p. 64.

 CD 2 TRACK 72 **Listen/Look. Listen/Say. Copy. Listen/Say.**

1. A·**mer**·i·can

2. Cal·i·**for**·nia

___·_____·__·_____

___·_____·__·_____

__·_____·__·__·_____

___·_____·__·_____

__·_____·__·__·_____

__ __ __ _____

_____·__·_____·_____

 CD 2 TRACK 73 **Listen/Look. Listen/Say.**

1. A·**mer**·i·ca   America

2. We live in <u>America</u>.

3. A·**mer**·i·can   American

4. Here is the <u>American</u> flag.

TEACHER   *Top:* Follow instructions, p. 9, top. Voice each syllable distinctly. *Bottom:* Point to and read each word twice, first voicing each syllable distinctly, then reading the word normally. Do this again and have students repeat. Then have students read each word to you. Say each sentence and have students repeat.

**Circle: How many states are in <u>America</u>?**

13                          50                          100

**Circle the <u>American</u> flag.**

**Circle <u>California</u>.**

TEACHER   Have students read the question and circle the correct answer.

1. A**mer**ican flag

   __**mer**__can  flag

   A_____i_____  flag

   __ _____ican _____

   _____ _____

2. A**mer**ican **In**dians

   __**mer**__can **In**____ans

   Am____i_____ ____di_____

   ____ **mer**i_____ **In**____ _____

   _____ _____

⊙ **CD 2 TRACK 75**   **Listen. Write.**

1. _____       4. _____

2. _____       5. _____

3. _____

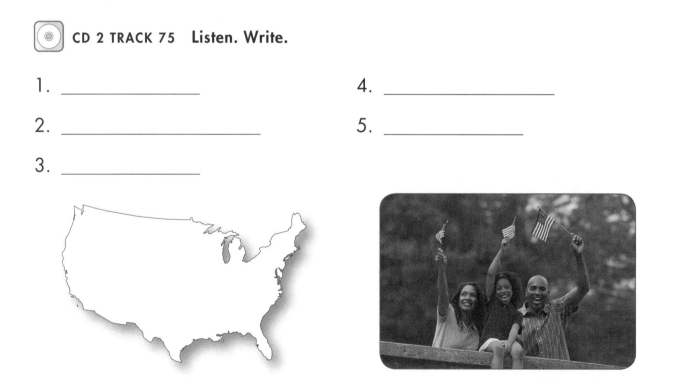

**Write the months.**

| January | | | | | | |
|---|---|---|---|---|---|---|
| | | | | 1 | 2 | 3 |
| 4 | 5 | 6 | 7 | 8 | 9 | 10 |
| 11 | 12 | 13 | 14 | 15 | 16 | 17 |
| 18 | 19 | 20 | 21 | 22 | 23 | 24 |
| 25 | 26 | 27 | 28 | 29 | 30 | 31 |

| F_ _ _ _ _ _ _ | | | | | | |
|---|---|---|---|---|---|---|
| 1 | 2 | 3 | 4 | 5 | 6 | 7 |
| 8 | 9 | 10 | 11 | 12 | 13 | 14 |
| 15 | 16 | 17 | 18 | 19 | 20 | 21 |
| 22 | 23 | 24 | 25 | 26 | 27 | 28 |
| | | | | | | |

| March | | | | | | |
|---|---|---|---|---|---|---|
| 1 | 2 | 3 | 4 | 5 | 6 | 7 |
| 8 | 9 | 10 | 11 | 12 | 13 | 14 |
| 15 | 16 | 17 | 18 | 19 | 20 | 21 |
| 22 | 23 | 24 | 25 | 26 | 27 | 28 |
| 29 | 30 | 31 | | | | |

| April | | | | | | |
|---|---|---|---|---|---|---|
| | | | 1 | 2 | 3 | 4 |
| 5 | 6 | 7 | 8 | 9 | 10 | 11 |
| 12 | 13 | 14 | 15 | 16 | 17 | 18 |
| 19 | 20 | 21 | 22 | 23 | 24 | 25 |
| 26 | 27 | 28 | 29 | 30 | | |

| M_ _ | | | | | | |
|---|---|---|---|---|---|---|
| | | | | | 1 | 2 |
| 3 | 4 | 5 | 6 | 7 | 8 | 9 |
| 10 | 11 | 12 | 13 | 14 | 15 | 16 |
| 17 | 18 | 19 | 20 | 21 | 22 | 23 |
| 24 | 25 | 26 | 27 | 28 | 29 | 30 |
| 31 | | | | | | |

| J_ _ _ | | | | | | |
|---|---|---|---|---|---|---|
| | 1 | 2 | 3 | 4 | 5 | 6 |
| 7 | 8 | 9 | 10 | 11 | 12 | 13 |
| 14 | 15 | 16 | 17 | 18 | 19 | 20 |
| 21 | 22 | 23 | 24 | 25 | 26 | 27 |
| 28 | 29 | 30 | | | | |

| J_ _ _ | | | | | | |
|---|---|---|---|---|---|---|
| | | | 1 | 2 | 3 | 4 |
| 5 | 6 | 7 | 8 | 9 | 10 | 11 |
| 12 | 13 | 14 | 15 | 16 | 17 | 18 |
| 19 | 20 | 21 | 22 | 23 | 24 | 25 |
| 26 | 27 | 28 | 29 | 30 | 31 | |

| August | | | | | | |
|---|---|---|---|---|---|---|
| | | | | | | 1 |
| 2 | 3 | 4 | 5 | 6 | 7 | 8 |
| 9 | 10 | 11 | 12 | 13 | 14 | 15 |
| 16 | 17 | 18 | 19 | 20 | 21 | 22 |
| 23 | 24 | 25 | 26 | 27 | 28 | 29 |
| 30 | 31 | | | | | |

| S_ _ _ _ _ _ _ _ | | | | | | |
|---|---|---|---|---|---|---|
| | | 1 | 2 | 3 | 4 | 5 |
| 6 | 7 | 8 | 9 | 10 | 11 | 12 |
| 13 | 14 | 15 | 16 | 17 | 18 | 19 |
| 20 | 21 | 22 | 23 | 24 | 25 | 26 |
| 27 | 28 | 29 | 30 | | | |

| O_ _ _ _ _ _ | | | | | | |
|---|---|---|---|---|---|---|
| | | | | 1 | 2 | 3 |
| 4 | 5 | 6 | 7 | 8 | 9 | 10 |
| 11 | 12 | 13 | 14 | 15 | 16 | 17 |
| 18 | 19 | 20 | 21 | 22 | 23 | 24 |
| 25 | 26 | 27 | 28 | 29 | 30 | 31 |

| N_ _ _ _ _ _ _ | | | | | | |
|---|---|---|---|---|---|---|
| 1 | 2 | 3 | 4 | 5 | 6 | 7 |
| 8 | 9 | 10 | 11 | 12 | 13 | 14 |
| 15 | 16 | 17 | 18 | 19 | 20 | 21 |
| 22 | 23 | 24 | 25 | 26 | 27 | 28 |
| 29 | 30 | | | | | |

| December | | | | | | |
|---|---|---|---|---|---|---|
| | | 1 | 2 | 3 | 4 | 5 |
| 6 | 7 | 8 | 9 | 10 | 11 | 12 |
| 13 | 14 | 15 | 16 | 17 | 18 | 19 |
| 20 | 21 | 22 | 23 | 24 | 25 | 26 |
| 27 | 28 | 29 | 30 | 31 | | |

TEACHER Have students fill in the blanks to spell the names of the months.

**CD 2 TRACK 76  Listen/Look. Listen/Say. Copy. Listen/Say.**

1. Memorial Day is in May.

   _____ _____ _____ _____ _____.

2. Independence Day is in July.

   _____ _____ _____ _____ _____.

3. Presidents' Day is in February.

   _____ _____ _____ _____ _____.

4. American Indians lived here first.

   _____ _____ _____ _____.

5. California has the most people.

   _____ _____ _____ _____ _____.

**CD 2 TRACK 77  Read-alouds.**

1. When is Independence Day?

2. When is Memorial Day?

3. Why do people come to America?

4. What are the colors of the American flag?

TEACHER  *Top:* Follow instructions, p. 12, bottom. ***Bottom:*** Follow instructions, p. 43, bottom.

1. _____ _____ _____ _____ _____.

2. _____ _____ _____ _____ _____.

3. _____ _____ ___ _____ _____.

4. _____ _____ _____ _____ _____.

5. _____ _____ _____ _____.

TEACHER   *Dictation:* 1. Memorial Day is in May.  2. Independence Day is in July.  3. Presidents' Day is in February.  4. American Indians lived here first.  5. California has the most people.

Section 13   **105**

# Question Words
## (for reading practice)

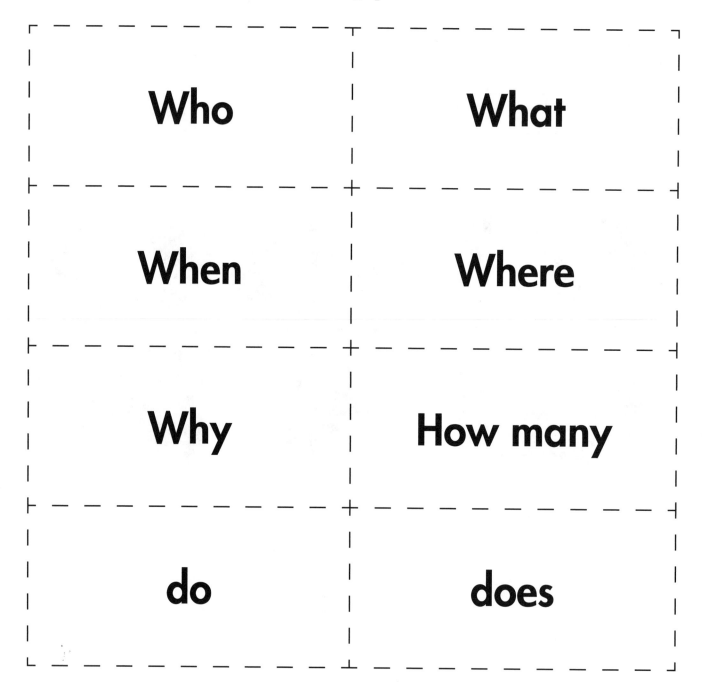

Who

What

When

Where

Why

How many

do

does

TEACHER  Follow instructions for word cards in the *Teacher's Guide*, p. 45.